Forgotten TV

Forgotten TV
101 TV Shows You've Probably Never Heard Of

by

Kevyn Knox

Experimental Forest Press

Copyright © 2020 Kevyn Knox & Experimental Forest Press

A to Zooey Productions

ISBN: 978-1-7350889-0-7

All Rights Reserved

First Edition

Experimental Forest Press
1333 Bartine Street
Harrisburg Pa 17102

123456789

Thanx to Noelle Craig for all Her Help!!

@kevynknox on Facebook, Instagram, & Twitter

**Dedicated
to**

**My Grandmother
Anna Margarette Knox
For indulging my TV obsession as a youth**

And

**My Wife
Jeanette Amy Trout
For indulging my TV Obsession as an adult**

Introduction

Since broadcast television first made it on the scene in the 1940's, all the way through to this brave new world of TV that has expanded well past the old network style of the past five decades, even expanding past the actual TV itself, there have been many great, and fondly remembered shows. Shows like *I Love Lucy, Dragnet, Leave it to Beaver, Star Trek, All in the Family, The Love Boat, Cheers, NYPD Blue, The Simpsons, Friends, The Sopranos, The Office, Breaking Bad, Modern Family, Game of Thrones*, and dozens and dozens and dozens of others. But we didn't come here to talk about these shows – these fondly remembered shows. No, we are here today to talk about all those shows we don't remember. Or at least, all those shows you don't remember. Obviously, I remember them. I'm writing about them. But I digress.

But even those shows I do remember, some are mere cobweb memories, some are perhaps by name only. In one way or another they are forgotten to some degree – even by this author. This book highlights 101 of those forgotten, or at least semi-forgotten shows. But all forgotten shows are not all forgotten in the same way. There are those shows that were popular once upon a time, but due to a lack of preservation via the networks, or a loss of tapes in a fire or some such tragedy, are relatively unknown today. There are those shows that were quality shows, but just never found their niche, and maybe were ahead of their time, or ran up against a ratings behemoth like *Dallas* or *60 Minutes*, and are sadly forgotten today. Then there are those shows that were just godawful fiascos. These shows, some of which lasted just one episode, have no right to be remembered, and probably should be forgotten - but thanks to me, I won't let you forget them. Obviously there are going to be shows on here that you remember from growing up or that you recognize from another life – every person has a different life, so every person forgets and remembers different things – but for the most part, these are shows you've probably never heard of, or only faintly recall in some sort of cobweb memory.

Whatever the case may be, here they are, all 101 of them, ranging from the earliest days of television, aka 1949 and the first ever network sitcom, a show that inspired every family sitcom that came after it, even *I Love Lucy*, all the way up to the past decade, and more modern, but equally forgotten shows. You'll find comedies and dramas, variety shows and game shows, science fiction and reality TV. You'll find shows starring future household names and shows where careers were ended because of the ridiculousness of their shows. You'll find big name producers and successful TV mavericks stinking up the place with some of their more dubious attempts at creation. You'll find inexplicable premises and unexplainable attempts at spinoffs. You will even find a show about Adolph Hitler living next to Jewish neighbors in the 1938 Berlin suburbs, all done like a remake of *I Love Lucy.*, replete with laughable laugh track.

Yeah, really. That's one of the shows that lasted just one episode and most likely destroyed the reputation of all involved. And you can read all about it, and 100 other shows in this book. A book of TV criticism, where you get 101 TV show reviews for the price of one, but also a look at television history and the people who made it all happen, from then until now. But more on that later in the book. For now, just read on and enjoy. I'll see you again later.

Mary Kay and Johnny (1947-50)

A groundbreaking sitcom about a moderately straight-laced husband and a wacky and wonderful wife, played by a real life married couple? Hold on, because this may not be the show you're thinking of. Not to take anything away from the success and influence of the great classic situation comedy, *I Love Lucy*, which is considered by many to be the Rosetta Stone of the modern situation comedy, the grand dame of them all, if you will, but there was a show that came before it, a show that actually influenced Lucille Ball and Desi Arnaz, Jr. to create their own series, and become that successful and highly influential show. That show, which debuted on the old DuMont Network on November 18, 1947, nearly four years before Lucy and Ricky came on the scene, was *Mary Kay and Johnny*. It is considered the first situation comedy to be broadcast on US television, and its basic format has been repeated and reproduced hundreds of times throughout television history, including, and most famously, by the aforementioned *I Love Lucy*.

The plot centered around a bank employee and his zany wife, living their lives in New York City. The show was created and written by Mary Kay and Johnny Stearns. The couple had just been married the year before their show made it's debut. He was 31. She was 22. The show was groundbreaking in so many ways. Other than just being the first sitcom on US television, it was also the first program to show a couple sharing a bed, and the first series to show a woman's pregnancy on the air. Another thing it beat *I Love Lucy* too. On December 31, 1948, the two weeks old

Christopher Stearns made his television debut, five years prior to Little Ricky making his debut appearance on *I Love Lucy*. After a year on Dumont, the show moved over to NBC, then to CBS for a few months, airing every weeknight, before heading back on over to NBC, where it ran until it's final episode on March 11, 1950.

The show was critically acclaimed at the time, but since the A.C. Nielsen Company did not start gauging ratings until 1950, there was no real way to know the true popularity of the show. Then an idea was hatched between the network and Anacin, who were the show's sponsors. During one live commercial spot, Anacin promised a free pocket mirror to the first 200 viewers who wrote in requesting one. As a precaution, the network purchased 400 mirrors, just in case the audience was bigger than they thought. A week later, they had nearly 9000 requests for mirrors, and that after just one commercial spot. So, it was official, with or without ratings, the show was a hit. As I stated earlier, the show was also critically acclaimed, and this author must take the critics words for this. Why? Because I've never actually seen the show. I know, I'm writing on it, but seriously, other than one tiny clip, I have never seen this classic sitcom. In fact, I would hazard a guess that not many others out there today have either.

Sadly, it is all too true, one cannot actually watch an episode of this groundbreaking show. Before 1948, Dumont broadcast their shows live and unrecorded. After that they did still broadcast live, but they did record on kinescopes in order to be shown, with some delay, on the West Coast. But alas, in 1975, Metromedia, who were the corporate successor to the Dumont network, famously disposed of the entire Dumont back catalog by tossing it into the East River. The episodes which aired on CBS and NBC are believed lost as well. The Paley Center for Media does have one 1949 episode in their collection, but the general public can no longer watch the show. I suppose this accounts for the show's forgotten status. Quite sad indeed.

The Goldbergs (1949-56)

There were a lot of TV shows from the early days of television that are forgotten now. Between the lack of preserving many of these early shows for posterity (the medium of television was thought of as a fad by most people of the day, including many of those working inside of it - hence not saving any recordings of many shows) and the haphazard way of tossing show after show at the small screen, much in the same manner as Jackson Pollock splattering paint upon his canvas, and moving onto the next idea almost immediately, the vast majority of shows from this so-called golden age, are almost completely forgotten today.

Sure, there were hit shows of the day that are still fondly remembered, but for every *I Love Lucy* there were a dozen or so shows like *Norby* and *Leave it to Larry* and *Joe & Mabel*. For every *Dragnet* there were shows such as *The Amazing Mr. Malone* and *The Prudential Family Playhouse*. Even successful shows of the early 1950's, shows like *The Red Skelton Show, You Bet Your Life*, and *Our Miss Brooks*, are not known by many people today. This was proof that fame at the time does not equate to a long shelf life. In fact, there was one show from this time period, which ran off and on from 1949 through 1956, that was actually almost as popular as *I Love Lucy*. Back in the day, the name Molly Goldberg was as much a household name as that of Lucy Ricardo. Nowadays though? Well, this is a book about forgotten TV after all.

The show in question is *The Goldbergs*, and it was the brain child of writer-actress Gertrude Berg. Originating on radio in 1929, Berg wrote, directed, and starred in every episode. It was a weekly show until it turned to daily episodes in 1931, and would run on NBC, and later CBS radio until 1946. *The Goldbergs* (originally titled *The Rise of the Goldbergs*) ran longer than any other comedy in radio history, save for *Amos & Andy*. In 1949, Berg brought her loving Jewish mother and former hit radio show to CBS television. Audiences had heard Molly Goldberg shout "Yoo-Hoo, Mrs. Bloom!" to her neighbor across the way for years on the radio, but on January 10, 1949, those audiences could finally put a face to that voice. The show what such an immediate hit on television, that in 1950, Berg and co-star Philip Loeb as hubby Jake Goldberg, filmed a big screen version of the show. This may be the very first crossover into movies that television ever did. In January 1951, Gertrude Berg won the very first Best Actress Emmy Award. But alas, a few months later, CBS dropped the show after Berg, who owned the rights to both the TV and radio versions of her show, refused to fire her friend Philip Loeb after he was blacklisted for being a communist by the (very Un-American) House Un-American Activities Committee. It was the 1950's in Hollywood, and the witch hunt was on.

The following year, NBC said they would pick up the show for the 1952-53 season, but only on the stipulation that Berg fire Loeb. After getting the okay from Loeb himself, who wanted his friend to succeed, Berg gave the part of her TV husband to Harold Stone (who was later replaced by Robert H. Harris) and the show began airing its third season as a twice-weekly, 15 minute show in the Fall of 1952. In 1954, with a move to the Dumont Network, the show went to a 30 minute format, but was shortly cancelled due to money problems at the failing Dumont. A final version of the show ran in syndication from 1955 to 1956. Tragedy soon came though. Due to depression from being blacklisted, and thus an inability to find work in the industry he once loved, Philip Loeb took his own life on September 1, 1955. On a sidenote, even after his removal from the show, and right up until his death, Berg never stopped paying her friend and former TV husband a weekly salary. Even though the powers that be were on a witch hunt, Berg would have no part of it.

As for the legacy of this long forgotten, but well loved show, *The Goldbergs* were televisions first Jewish family, which made it groundbreaking in its treatment of Judaism in mid-century America. One Jewish educator, in a paper titled "The Jewish Mother," said of Berg's series, "This series has done more to set us Jews right with the `goyim` than all the sermons ever preached by the Rabbis." Unfortunately, network TV would not see another major Jewish character until Bernie made the mistake of loving that shiksa Bridget in 1972. Meanwhile in 1959, Berg won a Tony Award for Best Actress for her performance in *A Majority of One*. Then in 1961, Berg found herself back on regular series TV, on the sitcom *Mrs. G. Goes to College*, retitled *The Gertrude Berg Show* midway through it's one and only season on CBS. Berg, in this new sitcom, was playing pretty much just a newer version of her old Molly Goldberg character – but apparently not near as successfully. There is a show on ABC today titled *The Goldbergs*, but is similar in name only. Berg passed away in 1966, and her show, which was one of the biggest hits, and most beloved shows of its time, eventually fell through the cracks of television history, and today is a sadly forgotten gem.

The Beulah Show (1950-53)

Just like the contemporaneous *Amos 'n' Andy* over on CBS, the ABC series *The Beulah Show* had its lifespan cut short by protests from critics, including the NAACP. And rightly so. But more on that later. Right now, let's look at the long long history of Beulah. That history actually predates the television show. Originally portrayed by a white male actor, Marlin Hurt, which was almost always the case back in the day, Beulah Brown first appeared in 1939 when Hurt introduced and played the character on the *Hometown Incorporated* radio program. After appearing on several different radio programs, Hurt took his character to the popular *Fibber McGee and Molly* radio show in 1944, before branching out on his own on *The Marlin Hurt and Beulah Show* in 1945. After Hurt passed away in 1946, Bob Corley, another white actor, took over the role on the newly minted radio show, *The Beulah Show*.

Then, on November 24, 1947, Hattie McDaniel, Academy Award winner for *Gone with the Wind*, took over the role. The actress, an actual African-American woman, was finally playing the part of Beulah Brown. McDaniel was getting $1000 a week and managed to double the ratings. Her casting also made the NAACP happy, as she was the first ever black woman to star in a network radio program. McDaniel continued in the role until she became ill in 1952 and was replaced by Lillian Rudolph, who in turn was eventually replaced by her sister, Amanda Rudolph. After nine years on CBS radio, the show went off the air in 1954.

But we're not here to talk about the radio show. We're here to talk about the TV show that ran on ABC from 1950 to 1953.

In 1950, while the show was still bringing in listeners over on the radio, Roland Reed Productions adapted the property into a TV situation comedy for ABC. The premise of the show was that Beulah was a maid working for the Hendersons, a middle class white family, consisting of Harry and Alice, and their young son Donnie. The show also featured Beulah's boyfriend Bill Jackson, and Oriole, the maid from next door and Beulah's dimwitted BFF. Although these were the core characters through all three television seasons, the cast was far from a set thing.

The first season, 1950-51, was filmed in New York, and starred Ethel Walters, who was also concurrently appearing on Broadway as Berenice Sadie Brown in Carson McCullers' *The Member of the Wedding*, a part she would play a year later in the movie version. Percy "Bud" Harris played Bill, until he quit in 1951, in frustration of having to play an "Uncle Tom" character. Harris was replaced by Dooley Wilson (Sam of *Casablanca*) for the remainder of the first season. Meanwhile, Butterfly McQueen, McDaniel's co-star in *Gone with the Wind*, played the part of simple-minded Oriole. But then the second season got an entire overhaul.

In season two, the show's production was moved to Hollywood, and the cast was completely replaced by the current radio cast. Hattie McDaniel took on the role of Beulah, while simultaneously playing the part on radio. The radio Bill and Oriole, Earnest Whitman and Ruby Dandridge, respectively, took over for their TV counterparts. McDaniel fell ill in 1952, and had to quit both the radio and TV versions of the show. Sadly, McDaniel, the first African American to win an Oscar, passed away after a short battle with breast cancer in October of that year. And just like that, we lost one of the greats. She was replaced by Louise Beavers, who would play the role until the show went off the air in 1953. The Henderson family were also recast after the move from New York to L.A., but the show was never really about them anyway, acting as just another generic sitcom family of the day.

In all, a total of 87 episodes were produced of *The Beulah Show*, but after it's cancellation, these episodes would only see the light of syndication for a short while, a syndication that other shows of the day like *I Love Lucy* and *Ozzie & Harriet* thrived in by the latter part of the decade. Even though Beulah was portrayed as probably the smartest character in the bunch, the NAACP blasted the show for it's stereotypical portrayal of African-Americans on TV, and just like the more famous *Amos & Andy*, it's syndication run would be cut short, and by the end of the decade, it would rarely ever be seen on television again. Sure, there are aspects that made Beulah seem like a strong woman, just like there were positive portrayals of people of color in *Amos & Andy*, but overall, it was a racist mess. Yeah, it was a step up from being portrayed by white actors, like both shows were on radio (*Amos & Andy*'s whitewashing lasted longer than the somewhat more progressive *Beulah*), but not a far or fast enough step. Therefore *Beulah* has been mostly lost and forgotten in television history.

Tales of Tomorrow (1951-53)

Everyone knows and remembers *The Twilight Zone*, which ran on CBS from 1959 to 1964, and which has been remade and retooled a multitude of times over the decades. A show as beloved and acclaimed (and remembered) has no place in a book such as this, nor does *The Outer Limits*, which ran on ABC from 1963 to 1965, and which also has been remade and retooled several times over the decades. But before these two groundbreaking sci-fi and horror anthologies hit the small screen, there was another show that was doing what these shows would later famously and more successfully do. The ABC series *Tales of Tomorrow*, ran for two seasons from 1951 to 1953, and featured stories by Arthur C. Clarke, Jules Verne, and other big names of the genre. This series, though not as well done as the aforementioned *Twilight Zone* (but then what anthology series ever was), paved the way for these later shows to follow.

Unlike most science fiction of the day, which was geared toward children, *Tales of Tomorrow* was a show for adults. These were serious dramatic takes on classic and contemporary science fiction stories. The first of its kind. The series featured the likes of Boris Karloff, Veronica Lake, Bruce Cabot, Thomas Mitchell, Rod Steiger, Lee J. Cobb, Cloris Leachman, Leslie Nielsen, and even Lon Chaney Jr. as Frankenstein's Monster. Shown live each week, the episodes were a bit primitive (and rushed with just a half hour to squeeze in stories like *Frankenstein* and *20,000 Leagues Under the Sea*) compared to *The Twilight Zone*, but they were still solid tales of the strange and unusual, featuring great acting from some of the greats of cinema. A radio version ran for a short time during the TV show's run. But alas, the series has not survived the sands of time like *The Twilight Zone* has, though it may be a bit unfair to compare this series, or any series really to one of the greatest shows to ever grace the small screen. For what it's worth, *Tales of Tomorrow* is a show that should be rediscovered, if not for anything else, for the important part it holds in television history.

Life with Elizabeth (1951-55)

Long before she was the sassy octogenarian Elka Ostrovsky on TV Land's original hit series, *Hot in Cleveland*. Well before she was the sweet but simple Rose Nylund on the 1980's NBC hit series, *The Golden Girls*. Even before she was the ever so snarky perfectionist, Sue Ann Nivens on *The Mary Tyler Moore Show*. Yes, long before all of these iconic roles, the one and only Betty White was already a bonafide television regular, and pretty much had been since the earliest of the early days. Besides her numerous gigs on the game and talk show circuit of the day (she was a regular on *Password, What's My Line, To Tell the Truth, The Jack Paar Show*, and *Match Game*), Betty White was the star of one of the wittiest situation comedies of the so-called Golden Age of Television. But alas, in keeping with the theme of the book, this wittiest of situation comedies was destined to become all but forgotten in the nearly sixty years since it last aired.

The name of this wittiest of situation comedies was *Life With Elizabeth*, which began life in 1951, as a live local production on KLAC-TV in Los Angeles, where White and TV husband Del Moore were on staff, before going into nationwide syndication for two seasons, beginning in 1953. Back in these early days of television, it was often an anything goes kind of time. With the new medium, new shows with new ideas were popping up all the time. Granted, this free-for-all led to a lot of rightfully forgotten experimentation in said new medium, in all genres, but it also led to odd little bits of brilliance, like *Life with Elizabeth*. Brilliant enough to garner Betty White the first of an eventual 21 Emmy nominations (and 5 eventual wins) when the show was first in syndication in 1951.

Based on the Elizabeth character White had created and performed on her improv show *Hollywood on Television*, *Life with Elizabeth* was a show about a zany housewife and her frustrated but loving husband, played by Moore. Jack Narz was the narrator and on-screen announcer, who, along with White would break the fourth wall, and speak directly to the audience. This quirky take, which is now a normal sitcom trope in shows such as T*he Office*, *Parks & Recreation*, and *Modern Family*, was way ahead of its time in 1953. One of these fun fourth wall breaking moments was when, after doing something to upset her husband, the announcer would ask, "Elizabeth, aren't you ashamed?" And White would slowly nod, but then, with a devilish grin, would vigorously begin shaking her head no no no. But it wasn't this ahead of its time aspect that got *Life with Elizabeth* axed in 1955. After 65 episodes, Guild Films who owned the show, chose to cancel the series because they thought having to many episodes would cheapen it's profitability in second run syndication. Betty White was sure to be okay though.

This is Your Life (1952-61)

The original concept of this show came to creator and host Ralph Edwards whilst he was hosting the game show *Truth or Consequences* on NBC radio just after World War II. Edwards had been asked to help out paraplegic soldiers by doing some sort of event for them. The radio host landed on the idea of putting these soldiers on the radio and showcasing their lives up until that point. In Edwards' words, he said he chose a "particularly despondent young soldier and hit on the idea of presenting his life on the air, in order to integrate the wreckage of the present with his happier past and the promise of a hopeful future." I think this would have just made me even more depressed, but hey, he did mention the "promise of a hopeful future," so who knows. Anyway, the idea for *This is Your Life* was born, and in 1948, the first episodes hit the radio waves on NBC.

After a four year run on NBC radio, Edwards, who was also producer, moved his show to NBC television. Each week, Edwards would surprise a person with their life. Reading from his big red book, Edwards would bring in long lost guests to thrill his audience, and hopefully his guests as well. People would get to see their third grade teacher again, or a childhood friend who moved away when they were still kids, or their grandmother who lived across the country, a country where cross-country travel was not nearly as easy as it is these days. The show was a hit, consistently high in ratings, and the recipient of two Emmy Awards, but let's face it, Edwards and his show were nothing more than a cheap publicity stunt and a disturbing invasion of privacy. Yes, some shows may have had good consequences, such as a 1954 episode where a woman talked of the charity she founded to raise money for her small town hospital, and viewers donated over $112,000 to the cause, but overall it was a maudlin attack on people's personal lives.

In one episode, Edwards had on Kiyoshi Tanimoto, a survivor of the atomic bombing of Hiroshima, and then had the unmitigated gall to bring on as a surprise from the man's past, the actual co-pilot of the Enola Gay, the plane that dropped that atomic bomb on Mr. Tanimoto's city. Talk about flagrant exploitation! Edwards angered many a celebrity too, most notably Stan Laurel, who was furious at Edwards, after he and former partner Oliver Hardy were tricked into doing an impromptu reunion on his show, the only television appearance of Laurel & Hardy, and the reason the duo refused to ever appear on television again. There was one celebrity though, that the show was forbidden to put on, and that was Ralph Edwards himself. The host had threatened to fire every member of his staff if they ever turned the tables and publicly presented his own life to him. Either he was hiding some pretty nasty skeletons in his own closet, or he knew just how horrible such a thing could be for a person. Or perhaps both. Called "the most sickeningly sentimental show on the air" by Time Magazine in 1960. A year later NBC cancelled *This is Your Life*. Edwards attempted a revival in 1971, but it didn't last. Another short-lived revival came in 1983, and a few other attempts were made in the 1990's and again in 2005, but nothing ever came of them. Today, as is per the requisite for this book, the show is long forgotten, and probably not in need of a look back into it's own exploitative life.

__Queen for a Day__ (1956-64)

"Would *you* like to be queen for a day?" This is how host Jack Bailey would open every show from it's beginnings on the Mutual Radio Network in 1945 to its TV run on NBC, and later ABC, from 1956 to 1964. This game show was similar to other shows of the era, like *Strike It Rich* on CBS, *Could Be You* on NBC, and *On Your Way* on Dumont, and later ABC (all of which could easily be included in this book), but as opposed to these shows giving out prizes for contestants answering quiz show questions, *Queen for a Day* gave it's prizes out to the contestant with the saddest story, all awarded by the oh so tried and true (and oh so accurate) result of an audience applause meter.

You see, the basic premise of this show was to get women to tell sad stories of their terrible lives, often times with them breaking down in tears, and then awarding prizes, everything from new refrigerators or washing machines to actual medical care for a sick child, all judged by the live studio audience. After the winning woman, the biggest sob story, was proclaimed Queen for a Day, she would be draped in sable-trimmed red velvet, topped with a bejeweled crown, and placed on a velvet upholstered throne. The show, which seemed to help a handful of wanting women (and kick to the curb all those ladies who's stories were not deemed pathetic enough for the live studio audience) but in reality it acted as the most demeaning of television shows.

Veteran TV writer Mark Evanier has called the program "One of the most ghastly shows ever produced." He further described it as "tasteless, demeaning to women, demeaning to anyone who watched it, cheap, insulting and utterly degrading to the human spirit." Yup, that about sums it up. I am sure there were legitimate hard cases on the show from time to time, but one guesses that the people who really needed the help, and not just the middle class contestants who were able to get on the show, were nowhere to be seen. This just added to the tasteless aspect of the show. This factor didn't really hurt the show's ratings though. Even though there was network skipping at play here, the ratings stayed solid, and it lasted 8 seasons on the air. After it's eventual cancellation, there were several attempted revivals and an actual musical version in 2012. Yup! Bailey would close each show with "This is Jack Bailey, wishing we could make *every* woman a queen, for every single day!" perhaps this is a show that should stay forgotten.

The Adventures of Superpup (1958)

Okay, to be fair, there is a solid reason why this show has been forgotten. It never actually aired – and hence it was never seen by audiences in order to be forgotten. But this show, or this would be show, as it were, is such an intriguingly weird specimen of television, that it just had to be included here. If it had aired, I believe it's ridiculousness alone would keep it in people's minds throughout the decades. You see, for six seasons, from 1952 to 1958, one of the more popular TV series was a show called *The Adventures of Superman*. Based on the DC Comics character created by Jerry Siegel and Joe Shuster, and starring George Reeves as Clark Kent (as well as that other guy) was the first television series adaptation of a superhero comic book. In 1958, the show went on hiatus after the death of actor John Hamilton, who played Perry White, with the intention of returning in 1959 for at least two more seasons. But alas, during this hiatus, Reeves died from a gunshot wound to the head. Some claim it was suicide, others that he had been murdered. The whole affair is still open for debate, and has, to this day, never been satisfactorily solved. But this is not a book about Hollywood scandals & unsolved mysteries, so we move on.

Between the time of what would end up being the final episode of *The Adventures of Superman* and the mysterious death of Mr. Reeves, another Superman inspired show would attempt to make it's way to the small screen. Attempt is the integral word in that sentence. It was at this time that comic book writer & editor, turned producer of *The Adventures of Superman*, Whitney Ellsworth, created a pilot that he hoped would cash in on the popularity of his other show, and maybe even work as a filler until production began again on *Superman*. Thus was born *The Adventures of Superpup*. That's right – Superpup. No, this was not a show based on Krypto the Superdog, a canine character who had just been introduced in the comics in 1955. This was the story of Superman, but Superman from an alternate dimension where everyone is an anthropomorphic dog. Yup. That's right.

In a precursory nod to the acid-induced creature features from the Sid & Marty Krofft shows that permeated children's television in the late 1960's and early 1970's, *The Adventures of Superpup* consisted of live actors dressed in some of the creepiest animal costumes this side of the aforementioned Krofft shows. But this was a good decade before we would ever see the cowboy boot wearing dragon known as H.R. Pufnstuf or the gallant little sea monster named Sigmund. Here we had Billy Curtis, best known as the star of the 1938 film, *The Terror of Tiny Town* (the first ever "Musical Western with an all Dwarf Cast"), in canine costume as Bark Bent, aka Superpup. The show also gave us characters such as Pamela Poodle, Terry Bite (played by Angelo Rossitto from the classic 1932 film *Freaks*), Sergeant Beagle, and a villain called Professor Sheepdip, who was played by Harry Monty, who did double duty as both a Munchkin and a flying monkey in *The Wizard of Oz*.

In the end, the pilot of this weirdly entertaining fiasco was not picked up, and is today mostly forgotten, save for those weirdos like me. The pilot was included as a bonus feature on the 14 disc DVD set of "Superman: The Ultimate Collection," and bits and pieces can be seen to be believed on Youtube, but outside of the morbid curiosity crowd or just your regular comic book loving weirdo (this author fully included), *The Adventures of Superpup* has been long forgotten, which still sounds a bit odd for a show that was never actually shown.

The Hathaways (1961-62)

It was a no-brainer. A show about a nice young suburban married couple who were raising three children. What could be more wholesome, more Middle America, more white picket fence than that? What could sell better in the day and age of the Cleavers and the Nelsons? In the era of *My Three Sons* and *Father Knows Best*? Oh, wait a minute. Did I mention the three children being raised by this young suburban married couple were actually a trio of chimpanzees known on the variety show circuit as The Marquis Chimps? Yeah. A trio of performing chimps. What could be more wholesome, more Middle America, more white picket fence than that? Maybe the word we're looking for is gimmicky. What could be more gimmicky than that?

The show was called *The Hathaways*, and for it's one and only season in 1961-62, it aired Friday nights at 8:00 on ABC, as the lead-in to *The Flintstones*. The premise, if not a bit ridiculous, was simple. The aforementioned young suburban married couple was Elinore and Walter Hathaway. He was a real estate agent and she was the era typical housewife. Oh yeah, and they were raising three chimpanzees as their own. But you already knew that. They were Charlie, Enoch, and little baby Cindy. The kids were adopted. Peggy Cass played Elinore. Cass was already an Academy Award and Golden Globe nominee for Best Supporting Actress for her performance in *Auntie Mame* in 1958. Character actor Jack Weston played Walter. Weston would go on to a steady career in supporting roles on both TV and in film, with roles in *Wait Until Dark*, *The Thomas Crown Affair*, and *Cactus Flower*. Later in his career he was Max Kellerman in the 1987 film *Dirty Dancing*. As for the chimps, they were already famous for their appearances with Ed Sullivan and Jack Benny, as well as several TV commercials.

Ratings for this Screen Gems production were so low that it's initial sponsor, Ralston-Purina backed out before the show had even run it's inevitable one season course. I suppose, through the almighty power of hindsight, these low ratings were to be expected. I mean, this was a show about a human couple raising three chimpanzees as their own, even so much as calling them their children. The show was cancelled after 26 episodes, and was never shown in syndication. Hence the totally forgotten outcome of *The Hathaways*. But ya know what? Judging from the episodes I have seen, I have to say I kinda liked the show. Sure, it may not be the top of the pops, but when compared to those shows from my opening salvo, shows like *Father Knows Best* or *Leave it to Beaver* or *My Three Sons*, it's not really as awful as the critics of the day have more than insinuated. Yes, it's just as corny as those overblown nuclear family comedies of the day, but the ridiculousness of chimp children sells it for me. *The Hathaways* may have been a show ahead of its time. Or maybe it's just me. Who knows?

I'm Dickens, He's Fenster (1962-63)

During the 1962-63 TV season, Leonard Stern, the legendary TV writer (*The Honeymooners, The Phil Silvers Show*) and future hit producer (the smart & savvy *Get Smart*), received many fan letters praising his one season wonder, *I'm Dickens...He's Fenster*. One of these letters was from a fan by the name of Stan Laurel. Stern was expected to believe that this was *the* Stan Laurel. But Stern wondered to himself, why this comedy legend, the creative genius behind all those old Laurel and Hardy films, would take the time and/or effort to write a fan letter, let alone several fan letters, as the case was, to a new, and as of yet unproven TV show? Why indeed? It had to be a joke. Stan Laurel was one of the great comic geniuses of cinema. He certainly would not bother with some little unknown sitcom on a third rate network. Or would he?

Then one day, while Stern was having lunch with old buddy, Steve Allen, the comic wondered aloud whether his friend had received any special fan letters lately. It was at this moment that Stern had figured it must have been his old pal playing a prank. I mean, really, why would someone like Stan Laurel bother with him. It must have been Steve Allen pranking his friend. Well, during the aforementioned luncheon, Allen told Stern that Stan Laurel had run into him, and wanted to know why he had never written back to the comedy team legend. What!? The letters were real!? Stan Laurel was a fan of his new show!? Yup, that indeed was the case. Laurel loved the smart slapstick that was the crux of the show. He really was a fan. Well, Stern wrote Laurel back, and the two became fast friends. Sadly, even the approval of Stan Laurel would not be enough to save this show from being a one season and done kind of show.

The show starred John Astin, two seasons before becoming Gomez Addams on *The Addams Family* and stalwart character comic actor Marty Ingels, who as a matter of trivia, would later on voice Pac-Man in the 1982 Hanna-Barbera cartoon. These two played Harry Dickens and Arch Fenster, a pair of bumbling carpenters, a la Laurel & Hardy, hence Stan Laurel's love for the show, and were great at it. The show also featured Emmaline Henry (later the wife of Dr. Bellows on *I Dream of Jeannie*) as Harry's wife. The show was filmed in front of a live studio audience, which, in that era, was unusual for a show not starring an already big name star like Lucille Ball or Dick Van Dyke. The show was definitely slapstick humour, full of silly antics and painful-looking pratfalls, but also took on more serious subjects like greed and social inequality, albeit in a comedic, non-preachy manner, another thing Stan Laurel loved about the show.

Actually, it wasn't just Stan Laurel who praised this new comedy. Critics from all over the nation were hailing *I'm Dickens...He's Fenster*, as the show of the new season. Time Magazine called it "The best new situation comedy," and the New York Times called it the "Surprise success of the television season." With the show's Friday night at 9:00 timeslot, which put it opposite of ratings hit *Route 66* on CBS and the popular *Sing Along with Mitch* on NBC, the ratings were never that great on the already struggling ABC network. After 31 episodes, ABC would cancel the show the week before it's 32nd and final episode, and it would finally win its timeslot for the first and last time. Perhaps ABC should have given it a second chance, and a second season, but then if they had done that we may never have gotten John Astin's beloved turn as the Addams' patriarch.

My Living Doll (1964-65)

In 1964, CBS launched a brand new situation comedy onto the airwaves. The show was part of the so-called escapist fare that was starting to become big that season. Along with shows like *Gilligan's Island*, *Bewitched*, *The Munsters*, and *The Addams Family*, *My Living Doll* played off of a fantasy style of storytelling. Unlike those other shows though, *My Living Doll* ended up being nothing more than a one season wonder, and is pretty much all but forgotten today, hence its inclusion in this book. In fact, of the 26 episodes filmed, only eleven survive today. Actually all 26 episodes, filmed on 35mm, were destroyed in a 1994 earthquake. The eleven surviving episodes were transferred to digital, using existing 16mm prints owned by collectors, and released as a DVD collection. But what exactly is *My Living Doll* all about, you may ask. Well, let me tell you.

Bought and aired by CBS, without the typical aid of a pilot, thanks to producer Jack Chertok's recent success with *My Favorite Martian*, another one of that so-called escapist programming, *My Living Doll* is the story of a prototype robot who escapes the military facility where she was created, and is taken in by a psychiatrist friend of the robot's creator. The hook here is that the robot, originally designated as project AF 709, but later renamed Rhoda, has the appearance of a beautiful woman, perhaps even the perfect woman. And to make that hook stick, the role was given to Julie Newmar, the woman who just two years later would take on the iconic role of Catwoman on the equally iconic ABC series, *Batman*. At the time though, Miss Newmar was little known, having appeared as a dancer in a few movie musicals (*The Band Wagon, Seven Brides for Seven Brothers*) and making a few guest appearances on the small screen (*The Phil Silvers Show, Route 66*), but she did have something going for her. She was a knock-out and the perfect choice to play Rhoda the Robot.

The main crux of the series revolved around Rhoda's attempts at fitting in with normal society, and her "keeper" trying to cover up the fact that she is a robot. To play Dr. Bob McDonald, her so-called keeper, they got Bob Cummings to come aboard. Cummings was already a big TV star at the time, his self-titled sitcom, which ran for four seasons, hadn't been off the air for all that long. Granted, at 54, the actor was probably a bit too old to play opposite the 30 year old Newmar, but then the show never did bring the human and the robot together. In fact, like most other shows at the time, *My Living Doll* was rather chaste, at least on the surface. With censorship being what it was in early 1960's television, the fact that this man had a nubile young sexy android living in his apartment, and he had to invite his sister to move in, in order to act as chaperon, says it all. Of course, as is often the case in movies and TV, the censors don't seem to catch everything.

The powers-that-be did nix a lingerie-clad Newmar for the opening credits, but still allowed her to be dressed in a sheet for the entire first episode. Also in that first episode, every time Bob is told that Rhoda will do anything he tells her to do, Cummings gets a look on his face that should have probably been censored as well. But even with these little bon mots, the show, as I stated earlier, was quite chaste in its approach to the subject of sex, even more so than *I Dream of Jeannie*, which began the following season over at NBC. And that was a show where poor Barbara Eden had to have her navel magically disappear, lest it incite lust in the hearts of the husbands and fathers of the Middle America viewing audience. The reason I bring up *I Dream of Jeannie*, is because *My Living Doll* was an obvious influence on that more successful show. A beautiful woman with no real knowledge of the modern world taken in my a hapless man who quickly finds himself comedically in over his head. The big difference, other than the latter show being a success, and still fondly remembered to this day, is that Jeannie and her beloved Major Nelson fell in love and would eventually get married. *My Living Doll* never had such a consummation. Heck, Bob Cummings, our possible robot lover didn't even stay with the show for its entire season long run.

After 21 episodes, Cummings broke his contract, and left the show. Rumor has it that it was due to his not getting along with Newmar, but the actress later denied that was ever the case. The show would go on for another five episodes, with Rhoda being "given" to Bob's womanizing neighbor and friend, while he left the country. After these final episodes, CBS decided to cancel the show due to poor ratings. The show was actually somewhat popular at the time, but because it was on opposite ratings hits such as *Bonanza* and *The Patty Duke Show*, the ratings were never high enough for CBS to give it a second chance in a second season. Of course this freed up the lovely Newmar to be cast in that aforementioned iconic Catwoman role the following year. Overall, the show had its moments, and it does not belong wallowing around in the lower depths like some of the shows in this book. Yeah, it may not have been one of the upper crust of 1960's comedies either, but it probably deserves to be remembered more than it has been.

My Mother the Car (1965-66)

When deciding to include the "classic" sitcom *My Mother the Car* in this collection of forgotten TV gems, I figured it was a no-brainer, but on second thought, this 1965 NBC comedy actually may not be all that forgotten after all. True, I am guessing not that many people around today have ever watched even one of the show's 30 episodes, but thanks to it being one of the greatest TV flops of all-time, at the very least, it's name is known in infamy. The show appears on nearly every list of the worst shows of all-time. In 2002, TV Guide proclaimed it to be the second worst show of all-time, behind only *The Jerry Springer Show*. Even though it was a 1928 Porter they used on the show, *My Mother the Car* was the Edsel of the television world. For that alone, this show will never be forgotten. But, since that unfortunate name recognition is all it's got going for it, we might as well discuss the show a bit while we're all here.

For those who know the show only from that aforementioned unfortunate name recognition, please allow me to bring you up to speed on the awfulness that was, is, and always will be, *My Mother the Car*. The show would premiere at the height of the fantastical sitcom renaissance of the mid 1960's. From talking horses (*Mr. Ed*) to suburban witches (*Bewitched*) to enslaved genies (*I Dream of Jeannie*) to airborne nuns (*The Flying Nun*) to madcap monsters (*The Munsters* & *The Addams Family*) and Martians (*My Favorite Martian*) to sexy robot women (*My Living Doll*, see last chapter), the 1960's was full of...well, it was full of something. In the midst of all this comedic fantasy came a show about a man's mother being reincarnated as a 1928 Porter automobile. The pilot episode has David Crabtree, played by Jerry Van Dyke, brother of Dick, one of the biggest stars on television at the time, coming across an old fixer-upper in a used car lot. As he sits in the driver's seat, a voice comes through the radio. It just so happens to be the voice of his long dead mother, voiced by legendary star of stage and screen, Ann Southern, telling him she has come back as a car, in order to help her hapless son through life. This was pretty much the show in a nutshell.

The show did have a good pedigree behind the scenes. Creators Allen Burns and Chris Hayward had already had a hit the year prior with *The Munsters*, and Allen would go on to create *The Mary Tyler Show* and *Rhoda*, while Hayward worked as a writer and producer on *Get Smart*, *Barney Miller*, and *The Rocky and Bullwinkle Show*. Writer James L. Brooks would end up working with Burns again, as co-creator on *The Mary Tyler Moore Show*, before going on to write for *The Simpsons*, as well as winning three Academy Awards for Writing, Directing, and Producing the 1983 film *Terms of Endearment*. There was also multiple Emmy Award nominee and Golden Globe Winner Ann Southern as the voice of mother/car. But alas, none of this talent, neither past nor present, was enough to make *My Mother the Car* anything more than the mediocrity that it was. But, thanks to it being "The Show That Will Live in Infamy," *My Mother the Car* will never really be forgotten. But here it is anyway.

It's About Time (1966-67)

On September 11, 1966, two years after *Gilligan's Island* made it's debut, and three seasons before *The Brady Bunch* would make it's own debut, saw the debut of *It's About Time*. All three shows were created and produced by TV legend Sherwood Schwartz. The first show lasted three seasons and is still a beloved sitcom to this day. The third show lasted five seasons and, it too, is still a beloved sitcom to this day. Sure, they may have their detractors (and be more than a bit silly) but they are surely well known and still popular, and still shown in syndication to this day. That middle show though? Not so beloved. Not so remembered. But still equally as silly.

The premise of this show is actually not that far removed from the aforementioned *Gilligan's Island*. With this show though, instead of seven castaways on a tropical island, we get a pair of astronauts accidentally traveling back in time and getting stranded in prehistoric times. In order to keep costs down, Schwartz used many of the same sets and props from his hit island show for his new prehistoric world. It's in this prehistoric world that our intrepid astronautic castaways, Mac McKenzie (Frank Aletter) and Hector Canfield (Jack Mullaney), meet the other stars of the show, your not so modern day stone age family. This cave family consisted of Shad and Gronk, played by veteran comic actors, Imogene Coca and Joe E. Ross. We also meet their kids, Mlor and Breer, and tribal chief Boss, and his lackey Clon. In the pilot episode, Coca's character is actually called Shagg, until the not-so-with-it powers-that-be at CBS were made aware of that word's connotations as sexual slang in the UK.

Airing on Sunday nights, as lead-in to *The Ed Sullivan Show*, the first few episodes did well in the ratings, but even that timeslot couldn't help once word got out that the show really wasn't all that good. In fact, word was the show was not just bad, but a complete and utter fiasco. After 18 episodes of pretty much the same tired scenarios of modern man vs. prehistoric dangers (including dinosaurs where no dinosaurs belong), and with no sign of the ratings getting any better, Schwartz decided to shake the show up a bit. He had his astronauts finally repair their rocket, and make their way back to the 1960's – with their favourite cave family in tow. The remaining 8 episodes revolved around the cave people trying to deal with modern society. Of course, this plot reversal, this same old same old attempt at making a scenario work, didn't really help the ratings at all though, and *It's About Time* was cancelled in the Spring of 1967, destined to become lost in time itself.

Occasional Wife (1966-67)

This NBC situation comedy, did not lead so much an occasional life, as it did a rather brief and unstoried life. Like many of the other shows in this book of forgotten shows, the show known as *Occasional Wife* did not last very long. It did however, unlike several of the shows in this book, actually manage to get a full season in, before having its plug pulled.

The story of the show goes a little like this: Peter Christopher, played by Michael Callan, is a swinging bachelor who has been denied promotion at his job because his boss is a big believer in marriage and family values. So, as is par the course for silly situation comedies of the day, Peter convinces a young hat check girl, Greta Patterson, played by Patricia Harty, who also happens to be his neighbour, to pretend to be his wife when his boss is around. Simple enough. Of course this led to wacky hijinks galore. We would regularly see Greta rushing down the fire escape from her 9th floor apartment to Peter's 7th floor pad whenever the boss would show up unexpectedly, which seemed to happen on the regular. As a fun running gag, Bryan O'Byrne plays a man living on the 8th floor, just silently watching the antics going up and coming down. He was credited simply as "Man in the Middle."

In the end, after all those wacky hijinks, NBC cancelled *The Occasional Wife*, in May of 1967. Peter and Greta never did get together, as one might have expected from such a storyline. Granted, if the show had survived to a second season, this very thing might have happened. Everyone loves a love story. Decades later, audiences fell in love with the on again, off again antics of Sam and Diane, Jim and Pam, and Ross and Rachel. But in 1966, this occasional husband and wife never did the "will they or won't they" dance. Well, at least not on screen. Off screen is a different story. Off screen, co-stars Michael Callan and Patricia Harty were married in 1968, just a year after their show was canceled. The marriage barely lasted longer than their series though, as they were divorced by 1970. Both marriage and show are now long forgotten.

Voyage to the Bottom of the Sea (1964-68)
The Time Tunnel (1966-67)
Land of the Giants (1968-70)

Long before he became the disaster king of Hollywood, with such motion pictures as *The Poseidon Adventure*, *The Towering Inferno*, and the bee-riffic *The Swarm*, Irwin Allen was a television producer of some of the most fantastical adventure series of the 1960's. Four fantastical adventure series to be exact – and all of them were hits of varying degrees. Only one of these four has stood the test of time though. *Lost in Space*, which ran for three seasons on CBS, from 1965 to 1968, is still a cult classic to this day. The show can still be readily found in syndication, as well as multiple different streaming services, and even on DVD – whatever that is these days. There was a movie adaptation, though we probably shouldn't bring that up, and a rebooted series which is actually quite spectacular (Parker Posey kills), and the show is a regular in many a best of all-time list. The point is, *Lost in Space* has no place being part of a book such as this. Allen's other three 1960's fantastical adventure series', though all popular in their time, and still cherished by the more astute sci-fi aficionado today, sadly do belong here. So let's discuss them, shall we?

The first up is *Voyage to the Bottom of the Sea*, based on Allen's 1961 movie of the same name. The show premiered on Monday, September 14, 1964, at 7:30 on ABC, and ran for four seasons on the network, making it Allen's longest running series, outlasting even *Lost in Space* by a year. The show, as can probably easily be ascertained by it's title, was an undersea adventure series. The brunt of the series took place aboard the Seaview, a nuclear submarine designed by retired Navy Admiral Harriman Nelson, played by Richard Basehart, best known at the time as "The Fool" in Federico Fellini's brilliant 1954 film, *La Strada*. The ship was captained by Capt. Lee Crane, played by David Hedison. To the public, the Seaview was merely an oceanographic research sub, but in reality it was a secret base of operations for a crew that defended the world from threats of all kinds – and I do mean all kinds.

The first season saw the crew of the Seaview take on Communists in a mostly cold war setting. Granted, these Russian agents were interspersed with episodes of flying saucers and even a monster or two, one of which involved a mad scientist in the Antarctic, who created monstrously large killer plankton. But even these more fantastical episodes were still based in some sort of grounded cold war type setting. Then came season two. Now being shot in full colour, the writers began coming up with more and more fantastical scenarios for our intrepid Seaview crew to encounter. The next three seasons saw mummies and werewolves and Nazi's back from the dead. There was one episode that saw Admiral Nelson and the crew battling a killer white gorilla. Incidentally, we would see this white gorilla again, as this gorilla suit, with added horn and dorsal spikes would later become the Mugato in the season two episode of *Star Trek*, "A Private Little War." He would again appear with Lucille Ball in an episode of *Here's Lucy*, the comedian's second of about a million attempts at recreating the magic of *I Love Lucy*. But I digress.

As I was saying, the episodes from season two on would become more and more ridiculous – but only in the most enjoyable manner. The show was sort of *Star Trek* underwater, only here, the crewmen unlucky enough to be garbed in red were no more in danger than anyone else. And speaking of *Star Trek*, just before the second season, James Doohan was offered the part of a new character, Chief Sharkey (the role that would go to Terry Becker) but the actor turned it down after being offered another role the very same week – that of another Chief, Lt. Commander Montgomery Scott, the engineering chief of the U.S.S Enterprise, on a new show called *Star Trek*. But again, I digress.

The episodes would keep becoming more and more fantastical, and more and more sci-fi. In one episode, we got to see Vincent Price and an army of murderous puppets. There were also killer toys and alien threats and menacing ghosts. There were frost aliens beneath the polar ice caps and lobstermen attacks. There was time travel too. There was even one fourth season episode that saw an evil leprechaun haunting the corridors of the Seaview. The show was a hot, but apparently not a big enough hit to stop it's inevitable cancellation, and in 1968, ABC pulled the plug on *Voyage to the Bottom of the Sea*, but Irwin Allen always had something else up his crazy sleeve. One of those things was *Lost in Space*, but as discussed earlier, we aren't here to discuss that classic (and well remembered) show. We are here to talk about Allen's next project, *The Time Tunnel*.

On September 9, 1966, coinciding with the start of the third season of *Voyage* and the second of *Lost in Space*, *The Time Tunnel* made it's debut on ABC. This new show was ostensibly set in the Arizona desert underground facility of Project Tic-Toc, a top secret organization studying time travel. More widely, the show was set everywhere and everywhen, as it follows its two protagonists after they become lost in time. These two time lost protagonists were Dr. Doug Phillips, played by Robert Colbert, best known as the third Maverick brother on *Maverick*, and Dr. Tony Newman, played by actor and top ten recording artist (as well as Moondoggie from the *Gidget* movies) James Darren. The cast also included former Miss America, Lee Meriwether, who had just come off of playing Catwoman in the *Batman* movie, as Dr. Ann MacGregor, one of the more stationary scientists at Project Tic-Toc.

"Two American scientists are lost in the swirling maze of past and future ages, during the first experiments on America's greatest and most secret project, the Time Tunnel. Tony Newman and Doug Phillips now tumble helplessly toward a new fantastic adventure, somewhere along the infinite corridors of time." And with that opening salvo, each episode began, and Doug & Tony were tossed about that swirling maze of past and future ages. From landing aboard the Titanic, in the pilot episode, just one day before that ship's infamous end to showing up at Pearl Harbor on December 6, 1941, Doug & Tony were witnesses of some of the greatest moments in all of history. Strange how the Time Tunnel of Project Tic-Toc never took our intrepid time travelers to regular old spots, like a random Tuesday afternoon in the South of France or Pearl Harbor on December 8, 1941. Nope, we just saw our heroes going from one day that will live in infamy to another. The Battle of the Alamo, D-Day, Iwo Jima, Custer's Last Stand, the Siege of Jericho just before the walls came tumbling down.

We also got to see our heroes hop into the future a couple of times too, saving the world from alien attacks and Russian agents on Mars. Still no warm Sunday evening in South Bend Indiana in the Summer of 1949, with nothing to do but sip on some lemonade and watch the bugs collect on the screen door. Yeah, that would be a pretty boring episode. I suppose that's why Doug & Tony were always launched into the fray of a major world event. But eventually that being launched into the fray, that being lost in a swirling maze of past and future ages, had to come to an end. That end came when an ABC executive managed to gather support amongst the other big wigs of the network, for a new show titled *The Legend of Custer*. Even though the ratings were relatively solid, ABC cancelled *The Time Tunnel* and replaced it with *Custer*, which went on to fail ever so dismally, both in ratings and in the skewering it received from critics.

The show's cancellation came as a surprise to Allen, and therefore we never got to see our lost heroes find their way back to the present day. In the end, aka the final episode, Doug & Tony find themselves aboard the Titanic once again. This return to the first episode adventure aboard the doomed ocean liner does sort of wrap things up though. Perhaps showing that time is not linear, but a never ending loop – a Moebius strip instead, with our heroes trapped in a never ending cycle of time and time again. Maybe next time around they can get to relax on that porch in 1949 South Bend Indiana, sipping lemonade and watching the bugs collect on the screen door. There were a couple aborted attempts at a remake, but the closest we would ever come to seeing *The Time Tunnel* again was on the obviously influenced by hit series *Quantum Leap*, which ran on NBC from 1989 to 1993.

After all three of Irwin Allen's shows left the air (*The Time Tunnel* ended in 1967, while *Voyage* and *Lost in Space* ended in 1968) the producer tried one more time. This new show by Allen was called *Land of the Giants*, and it made its debut on ABC on the night of Sept. 22, 1968. The show was simple enough. Set in the then future year of 1983, the series tells the tale of the crew and passengers of a sub-orbital transport ship called the Spindrift – a rather fortuitous moniker indeed. In the pilot episode, while making a run from L.A. to London, the Spindrift spins out of control and crash lands in another world. A world that looked a lot like Earth, only here everything was 12 times larger than anything on Earth, and our little heroes had to spend the next two seasons evading giant people who wanted to experiment on them, giant bratty children who wanted them as playthings, and a myriad of giant spiders, dogs, cats, and other scary ass things 12 times their size. Oh my. Hence the title, though since our crashlanded heroes were no longer on Earth, the show could have just as easily been titled, *Land of the Little People*. I suppose it's all in perspective.

In 1970, after two seasons of giant sized fun, ABC pulled the plug on the show, not because of bad ratings (they were solid enough) but because it just cost too damn much to produce. Granted, Allen was very budget conscious, using and reusing props and sets and stock footage throughout all four of his series' (as well as letting *Star Trek* borrow it's share now and again) but even that wasn't enough to save his shows, some of the most expensive programs on television at the time, from getting the proverbial axe. Cut to today, and outside of *Lost in Space*, and your regular bevvy of science fiction nerds (a group this author proudly belongs too) these shows are not that well remembered, or even known to succeeding generations.

At least we still have the Irwin Allen Rock & Roll. What's that, you ask? Originating as the Seaview Rock & Roll, it was the rather ridiculous, but quite entertaining way the crew of the Seaview flung themselves about a stationary set, making it look as if their sub was being tossed about. Allen played this trick in all of his shows, and it actually became a thing. The original *Star Trek* became famous for it, and it can still be seen in the sci-fi of today. But seriously, the Irwin Allen Rock & Roll aside, you should put this book down, after reading the rest of it of course, and sit down and watch these fantastical adventure shows of Irwin Allen, all of which can be found on streaming services and DVD.

Mr. Terrific (1967)
Captain Nice (1967)

On January 12, 1966, a show debuted on ABC that would change, albeit quite temporarily, the face of prime time television. That show was *Batman*. It starred Adam West and Burt Ward as the crimefighting pair known as the Dynamic Duo. Becoming an instant hit, *Batman* would usher in a renaissance of superhero programming. Well, okay, perhaps renaissance is too strong of a word. Sure, the mid to late 1970's would bring around a veritable slew of superhero shows. Shows such as *Wonder Woman*, *Spider-Man*, and *The Incredible Hulk*, even the *Six Million Dollar Man* and *Bionic Woman*, if you so care to include those two. But it would not be for several more years or so until these shows were hitting the airwaves. No, the so-called renaissance, for lack of a better word, of which I spoke, would hit television screens within a year of the Caped Crusader's TV debut. In fact, I can even pin down an exact date for this renaissance (really, we need a better word here!) to have happened. That exact date was January 9, 1967.

You see, as ABC's *Batman* was winning over viewers during its inaugural season, both NBC and CBS were rushing to get out their own superhero shows for the following year. And just like the *Batman* series, both networks were going the funny, as opposed to serious route. And then, on the night of January 9, 1967, *Mr. Terrific* premiered at 8:00 on CBS. Then at 8:30, NBC debuted *Captain Nice*. And then within one hour on a wintery Monday night, *Batman* had his competition, for what it was worth. Vastly different from one another, *Mr. Terrific* and *Captain Nice* were like night and … later that same night. You see, *Mr. Terrific* was about mild mannered Stanley Beamish (Stephen Strimpell) who is given a pill by the government which turns him into an inept, yet strangely effective superhero. Meanwhile, a half hour later on Monday nights, *Captain Nice* was the story of mild mannered Carter Nash (William Daniels) who creates a formula which turns him into an inept, yet strangely effective super hero. See, vastly different.

Granted, there were a few minor differences in the shows. The main one being the pedigree behind Captain Nice. The show was created by Buck Henry, who two years earlier had co-created *Get Smart*, and was produced by Jay Sandrich, who would go on to direct and/or produce dozens of TV shows, such as *The Bob Newhart Show, The Mary Tyler Moore Show, Soap, WKRP in Cincinnati, Benson, The Cosby Show*, and *Two and a Half Men*. *Captain Nice* also had the bigger star power on the screen. In addition to the aforementioned Daniels, who would later become a two time Emmy Winner for his role on *St. Elsewhere*, voice KITT the car in *Knight Rider*, and star as the hard-nosed yet beloved teacher on *Boy Meets World*, the show also featured Alice Ghostley, who despite being just three years his senior, played Carter's mother on the show, prior to her classic turns in *Bewitched* and *Designing Women*. As for the cast and crew of Mr. Terrific …well, who knows whatever became of them.

But then, in keeping with the vast differences between the shows, *Mr. Terrific* ended its run on May 8, 1967, just a week after *Captain Nice* aired its final episode. See, different by a whole week. Not the same shows at all. Both shows did get a bit of a cult following in years to come, especially once the days of the VCR got underway, and this love of their campy style did manage to keep these shows from being all that forgotten throughout the 1980's and 1990's. Of course now, in this day and age of forgetting the past wholesale, now they are pretty much all gone and forgotten. Two shows that bore no resemblance to one another whatsoever.

The Second Hundred Years (1967-68)

The premise is simple. The year is 1900. Guy leaves his pregnant wife to head north to Alaska, to join in the gold rush. Guy is lost in an avalanche. Guy is presumed dead. Cut to 1967, and the guy's now 67 year old son, and 33 year old grandson are living in Woodland Oaks, California. Now cut to another avalanche and, in the manner of Captain America, the discovery of the frozen but still quite living body of our intrepid gold miner. Now cut to the reunion between 67 year old son, 33 year old grandson, and 101 year old long lost dad. Oh, and since he was frozen in ice, the 101 year old long lost dad still looks 33, and must now adjust to life in 1967. See, simple as can be.

Here are some more detailed facts about ABC's *The Second Hundred Years*. Monte Markham played Luke Carpenter, the aforementioned 101 year old dethawed minor, as well as his own 33 year old grandson, Ken, while Arthur O'Connell played the 67 year old son/father, Edwin. In the pilot episode, a still befuddled Luke awakes in a hospital to find himself surrounded by modern contraptions and all kinds of crazy (in his mind) futuristic gadgets and doodads. This is pretty much the gist of all 26 episodes. Guy out of time, trying frantically to fit into modern society. Granted, the show was not all that good, and was critically lambasted to boot, but it had the added burden of going up against CBS's *The Beverly Hillbillies*, one of the most popular shows on television at the time, and coming off of back to back top ten seasons. The show was cancelled after just one season, never to be thought of again. Maybe in a hundred years, television archeologists can find this show frozen in the ice of TV obscurity, and thaw it back to life.

The Ugliest Girl in Town (1968-69)

On September 26, 1968, a show about a man who has to dress in drag in order to get an acting job, and the girl of his dreams, debuted on ABC. It was *Tootsie* long before *Tootsie* was *Tootsie*. It was *Victor/Victoria* before Victor ever became Victoria (or was that the other way around?). It was a comedy of love and cross dressing. It was also a comedy with very little actual comedy, which is probably why it only lasted a single season. But looking back, that was probably too long.

The synopsis goes a little something like this: Timothy Blair is a Hollywood talent agent who falls in love with Julie Renfield, a British actress who is visiting the US to shoot a movie. After the movie is finished, she returns to England, but alas, poor Timothy cannot afford to follow this newfound love of his life. Later on, Timothy gets a chance to see Julie again when his brother Gene asks him to pose for a magazine photography assignment. All Timothy has to do is dress as a hippie and pose for a quick photo shoot in the park. The photos are sent to a modeling agent in England who assumes they are of a woman and hires "her" for more photos. Looking at Timothy in drag, one wonders how this is even possible, but hey, it's a sitcom, so let's roll with it. Thinking this would be the only chance to be with Julie again, Timothy accepts the offer, dubs himself "Timmie" and heads to the UK. Hilarity ensues. Okay, that last part may be a lie, but I am fairly certain the writers 8ntended for hilarity to ensue.

The rest of the show revolves around Timothy and Timmie dealing with problems which arise in London. You know, things like using the wrong bathroom, having your wig fall off, hiding out from gangsters when your brother accrues gambling debts.

You know, the normal problems of a reluctant drag queen in 1960's swinging London. This last tidbit smacks of *Some Like It Hot*, but you know, without any of the actual comedy that came with that film. I am sure a bunch of other things happened too, but the show is just too forgettable to remember any of those things right now.

The New People (1969-70)

Thirty-five years before Jeffrey Lieber, Damon Lindlelof, and J.J. Abrams gave the world their intriguing yet often frustratingly convoluted desert island opus, *Lost*, Aaron Spelling and Rod Serling gave us a desert island spectacle of their own. But, where *Lost* ran for six seasons, was a hit in the ratings, received many accolades, including an Emmy for Best Drama Series in its debut season, and despite that finale, is still talked about today, *The New People* was a flop, ran for just 17 episodes before being canceled midway through its first and only season, never won any awards (not that it ever had time to do so), and is pretty much all but forgotten in the annals of television history. Of course, that last part is why the show is in this book, in the first place, wherein *Lost* has no need to be here.

The New People debuted on ABC, on September 22, 1969. It was one of a whole new revamped Monday night line-up on the network, scheduled to do battle with ratings beasts such as CBS's *Gunsmoke* and *Rowen & Martin's Laugh-In* on NBC. ABC's idea was to run their new music-variety program, *The Music Scene*, from 7:30 to 8:15, and follow this up with *The New People* from 8:15 to 9:00. This unusual 45 minute running time was meant to counteract viewers from changing the channel on the hour or half hour, as many were wont to do back in the day, when a better show was airing on another network. Unfortunately for ABC, this idea did not work out so well. *The New People* did moderately well at first, but in the so-called end, *Gunsmoke*, and especially *Laugh-In*, did not waiver, and both *The New People* and *The Music Scene* went belly-up in the ratings, and both were canceled in January of 1970, after just 17 episodes.

The premise of *The New People* was rather simple, in a manner of speaking. A group of forty or so college students were on a world tour, visiting some of the more underprivileged areas of the planet, when the US government orders them back home after many of the students begin building unrest in certain areas. In the pilot episode, we meet this group of rabble-rousing youngsters, as they are told they must head back home. Before long, the group's plane crash-lands on a supposedly deserted island somewhere in the South Pacific. All the older people, save for one, are killed in the crash, but not to worry, the remaining 'square,' played by Richard Kiley, will die off from his wounds soon enough, and before the pilot episode ends, these veritable kids will find themselves abandoned and alone, forced to fend for themselves, and if possible, build a whole new society. Soon, in the pilot episode as well, we find out that the plane has crash-landed on an old abandoned nuclear test site, complete with buildings, food, drink, weapons, even a piano, and for some reason, working dune buggies. There are even a bunch of life-size dummies sitting and standing around, just to add to the creepiness of the hapless group's situation.

In the first episode alone, we see racial tensions flare and a lynch mob sensibility already begin to foster itself. In later episodes, we see everything from socio-political discord to accusations of rape to power struggles and an inevitable battle of the sexes. Although there are forty some crashed students on the island, the show revolves around a main core of six. These six were all archetypes, or some might say stereotypes. You had the disenfranchised rich girl, the stubborn Southern redneck, the ex-marine turned pacifist, and the rebellious man of color. Granted, we did see other characters make their respective ways to the forefront, often played by guest stars who would go on to bigger and better things (Richard Dreyfuss, Tyne Daley, and Billy Dee Williams all appeared on here before stardom hit), but after their spotlight episode, these characters would disappear back into the crowd, never to be seen or heard from again. As the show progressed, the island's new inhabitants began living out a modern day, typically counter-cultural Lord of the Flies-esque lifestyle.

Though the show was given mostly good kudos from critics of the day, some had said that the show was merely a superficial look at the youth culture of the day and the problems inherent in 1969 America, and even though the show had an edgy quality to its presence, these detractors are, at least in part, correct in their assessment. Granted, the series was quite powerful at times, but there was, at least in hindsight, a by-the-book kind of storytelling to the show's aforementioned socio-political discord. At least once one gets past the pilot episode, which was a strong start to the series. This pilot episode was written by Rod Serling, under the guise of on-screen nom de plume John Phillips. Serling is also given co-creator status with producer Aaron Spelling, but this would be his only connection to the show. Serling would move on to create and produce *Night Gallery* that same year. In a 1969 interview with Cecil Smith of the Los Angeles Times, Serling said of the show, "That's Aaron Spelling's show. He brought me the idea and I wrote the pilot script. Beyond that, I have nothing to do with it."

Whether this series was an influence on *Lost* or not, is still debatable. Actually, with the show falling into almost universal obscurity, it's probably not all that debatable. *The New People* probably had no influence on the making of *Lost* whatsoever, and is mere wishful thinking on my behalf, that everything is interconnected in some way. *Lost* had actually been conceived by Lloyd Braun, after a visit to Hawaii, where he had thought of a cross between the hit movie *Castaway* and the reality show, *Survivor*. In an article in Entertainment Weekly, *Lost* producer Damon Lindelof joked about how if he had heard of the series, he would have used the name New People for the band seen in flashbacks, of character Charlie Pace. Sadly, Lindelof is in the majority when speaking of how forgotten *The New People* is today. You can find a version of the pilot episode, complete with the original commercials, on Youtube, but good luck finding the other 16 episodes anywhere. Perhaps a DVD release is in the show's future, but I wouldn't hold your breath.

Love, American Style (1969-74)

Love, American Style, Truer than the red, white, and blue. *Love, American Style*, That's me and you. And on a star spangled night my love, You can rest your head on my shoulder. Out by the dawn's early light, my love, I will defend your right to try. *Love, American Style*, That's me and you. What could be more American, especially in 1969, at the start of what would become known as the sexual revolution, than these star spangled words of love (and sex) sung by The Cowsills at the start of the newest member of the ABC Friday night line-up?

Taking it's name from the Oscar winning 1961 film, *Divorce, Italian Style* (and the 1967 American spoof, *Divorce, American Style*), *Love, American Style* was an hour long anthology series revolving around stories of love and romance, and what got the censors and prudish set of the day all riled up, sex sex sex. Sex sells and ABC proved that with this show. The show was nestled in at 10:00 (the hour of prime time after mom and dad had put the kids to bed) the ending to one of the biggest (and hippest) nights of prime time in television history, following *The Brady Bunch* at 8:00, *The Partridge Family* at 8:30, *Room 222* at 9:00, and *The Odd Couple* at 9:30. And it nestled in perfectly.

The show was set up as an anthology, with each segment about some sort of romantic entanglement, running the gamut from teenagers in love to philandering spouses. Between each segment were risqué interludes of burlesque and vaudevillian chutzpah. Many of these segments would be tried out by various producers as pilots for new shows. Some as intentional attempts at pilots, but mostly as segments repurposed after the fact, and mostly without any success. Two episodes did make it onto the prime time schedule as their own entities though.

The first came from an animated segment which aired on February 11, 1972. It would be turned into the Hanna-Barbera produced animated prime time series *Wait Till Your Father Gets Home*, which can be read all about a bit later in this very book. The second was aired just a few weeks later in season three, on February 25, 1972. The segment was originally called "Love and the Television Set," but after the success of the show that sprang forth from it, it would be changed for syndication to "Love and the Happy Days." In case you were a little slow today, and you didn't catch on, the show which emanated from this segment, was the long running ABC situation comedy known as *Happy Days* –

a show that definitely does not need to be included in this here book. But whatever became of *Love, American Style*?

The Nielsen ratings were never stellar, but they were solid over the first four seasons. Unfortunately these solid ratings plummeted over season five, and the show was cancelled in 1974. There were a couple attempts to revive the series. First as a daytime alternative to CBS's The Price is Right in 1985. This was cancelled after a few months due to the enormous popularity of the CBS game show competition. In the 1998-99 season, another attempt was made, this time involving Melissa Joan Hart, at the height of her *Sabrina the Teenage Witch* fame, as one of the stars, but was shelved after just one episode. The show did later run in syndication, but in half hour segments, eventually just leaving the air altogether and becoming forgotten by succeeding generations. But this was a fun, if not a bit dated, series, and should be watched and remembered by those willing to put in the time and fulfilling effort.

UFO (1970-71)

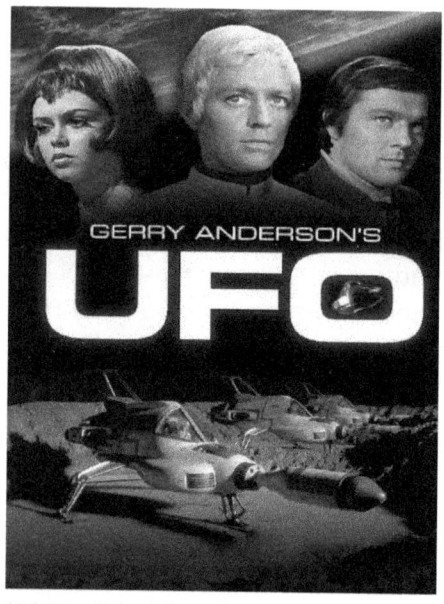

In 1960's British television circles, the names Gerry & Sylvia Anderson were synonymous with a thing called Supermarionation. This 75 cent word was the name that was given to the marionette puppets infused with electronic moving parts that The Anderson's used in all their shows. The husband and wife team became famous for the use of this unique form of visual storytelling in hit children's shows such as *Stingray* (1964-65), *Thunderbirds* (1965-66), and *Captain Scarlet and the Mysterons* (1967-68). Over the years, these series' have grown into cult status, with many modern day iterations of *Thunderbirds* on both film and TV, and have inspired many a copycat. In 1969, The Andersons created their first ever entirely live action (ie, no marionettes) work. This science fiction film was titled *Doppelgänger*, or *Journey to the Far Side of the Sun*, as it would later be known. It was set in the year 2069, and concerned the discovery of an alternate Earth on the opposite side of the Sun. A year later, in the Fall of 1970, The Andersons created their second live action work. This was the British television series, *UFO*, which ran for 26 episodes sporadically over the next few years, eventually crossing the pond to American television stations as well.

Using similar motifs, props, and costumes, as well as eleven of the same actors, from their previous live action experiment, *UFO* was the futuristic tale of a secret team of government agents

(Supreme Headquarters Alien Defence Organization, or SHADO) who protected Earth from invasion from outer space. The show wasn't all that futuristic though. You see, *UFO* was set in the far off future of 1980 – a mere ten years from when the show was filmed. Yet, even with not too far off future, we are given spaceships and lasers and the most fashion forward wardrobe imaginable. Apparently, we are meant to believe, in just a single decade, we went from the styles of mod London in 1970, to silver cat suit spacesuits and, for some odd reason, everyone wearing wigs. The women who ran the show's Moonbase (yeah, we had a Moonbase in 1980 – albeit a secret one) were dressed in skin tight silver space suits, wore a drag queen's worth of eye shadow, and all donned purple bob wigs. Apparently this was all the rage on the Dark Side of the Moon in 1980.

There is a simple explanation for all the wig wearing (many people on Earth, including the men, wore wigs as well – though none as electrifying as our Moon ladies in shocking purple) we got to see on *UFO*. You see, Sylvia Anderson had the idea that by 1980, wig wearing would be an everyday occurrence in society. Both women and men would don wigs all the time. It would be the fashion statement of the future, so The Andersons put it into their futuristic tale – perhaps to help sway the real world toward what Sylvia thought was inevitable. Now don't get me wrong, I love this idea, and would love to see wigs of all different styles and colours floating about on everybody's heads (my own included), but alas, outside of Andy Warhol and a few others from the fashion forward set, 1980 was not the great wig haven Sylvia Anderson had dreamed of. But I digress.

The biggest confusion from the show though, wasn't trying to figure out why people in the oh so near future were wearing wigs all the time (and again, let me say, I love this idea) but in the rather haphazard release schedule of the 26 episodes of the series. Owing to the fragmented nature of production at the ITV network in London, as well as a five month production break caused by the closure of MGM-British Studios, where the show was originally filmed (filming moved to Pinewood Studios after that), episodes, outside of episode one, were frequently broadcast out of order. This included different stations throughout England broadcasting them in varying order without seeming rhyme nor rhythm. This made for confusion when characters would die, and then suddenly appear again, as if back from the dead. It wasn't until the entire series was repeated on BBC Two in 1996-1997 that the episodes were shown in the proper order in the UK for the first time. Then again, the show was so convoluted, maybe nobody even noticed.

The star of the show, and the only character to appear in all 26 episodes, was Ed Bishop as Col. Edward Straker, Commander-in-chief of SHADO. Straker posed as a movie producer, whose studio was a front for the secretive SHADO. Bishop was a relatively unknown actor at the time, with a few small roles in a couple of James Bond films and a couple Stanley Kubrick pictures in his resume (bit parts in *Lolita* and *2001: A Space Odyssey*). And guess what? The brunette actor wore a white wig for the role. The show also featured George Sewell as Col. Alec Freeman, second banana at SHADO, and Gabrielle Drake as Lt. Gay Ellis, purple haired commander of the Moonbase. Both of these actors left the show midway through production, but thanks to the aforementioned haphazardness of broadcasting at the time, they still made appearances in "later" episodes. The fourth main cast member was Michael Billington as Col. Paul Foster, a pilot introduced in the second episode, who after witnessing a UFO attack, was asked to join SHADO. Billington, also a relative unknown at the time. Later on in his career, Billington found himself on the shortlist to become the new James Bond, when Roger Moore was questioning coming back for 1981's *For Your Eyes Only*. Sadly for Billington, Moore came back. Sadly for Moore, he also stuck around for *Octopussy* in 1983.

After the series had it's original haphazard run, network execs wanted a second series, and since the Moonbase heavy episodes were the most popular, the plan was to set them there, but this time even further into the future than a mere ten years. But, before anything but a proposal could be made, the plug was pulled on the idea of a second series. Eventually this proposal would be developed into a new series featuring the Moonbase, and entire Moon for that matter, being blown out into space. This series would be entitled *Space: 1999*, which ran for two seasons from 1975 to 1977, and became an even bigger hit in American syndication, due to the release of *Star Wars* while the show was still playing on independent channels throughout the nation. Of course, this series hasn't really stood the test of time either, and may, in a hint of foreshadowing, be included in a second or third volume of this book.

There were attempts at revivals of *UFO*, on both the small and large screens, but nothing ever came to fruition. Several of the props in the show, as way of futuristic predictions, did come to fruition though. Things such as everyday computer use, electronic fingerprint scanning and voice identification systems, and even a rudimentary DNA analysis of sorts. There were also depictions of cordless telephones used on the show, which did become a thing in the mid to late 1980's, but let's face it, it was the communicators from *Star Trek* that foreshadowed the invention of the cellular phones of today. Even Martin Cooper, the inventor of the cellular phone, a precursor to today's smart phones, says as much. Maybe that is why *Star Trek* is remembered but *UFO* is not. Yeah, there are probably other reasons too. Maybe it's the lack of wigs in everyday society.

Bridget Loves Bernie (1972-73)

This CBS comedy holds a rather dubious honor. With it's fifth place finish in the Nielsen ratings for the 1972-73 season (as well as being the top rated new show of the year) it holds the "honor" of being the highest rated show to be cancelled after just one season. Critically acclaimed and immensely popular in it's primest of prime time slots (Saturday night, nestled between ratings champs *All in the Family* and *The Mary Tyler Moore Show*), but still gone after just a single season. But more on this stupid decision in a bit. Right now, let's discuss the particulars of the show itself.

Bridget Loves Bernie was an adaptation of the 1922 play (and subsequent 1928 & 1946 films) called *Abie's Irish Rose*, written by Anne Nichols, about the turmoil revolving around the marriage of a Jewish man and an Irish Catholic woman. The show was created by playwright & screenwriter Bernard Slade, who was responsible for creating both *The Flying Nun* and *The Partridge Family*, as well as the hit play and movie, *Same Time, Next Year*. In this updated version, we meet a young Catholic teacher named Bridget (Meredith Baxter) and a Jewish cab driver named Bernie (David Birney) who fall in love at first sight and get married. The fun comes when the young newlyweds are forced to tell their respective parents about their surprise nuptials. These respective parents were played by Audra "Mrs. Roper" Lindley & David "Bosley from *Charlie's Angels*" Doyle (as Bridget's wealthy white bread parents) and Harold J. Stone & Bibi Osterwald (as Bernie's deli owning, down to Earth parents).

The writing in the show was witty and urbane, and the whole cast was good, but even that could not save the show from it's eventual demise. As I stated earlier, the ratings were more than fantastic, though to be fair, it's timeslot would have boosted any show's Nielsen's. Even Birney once conceded that, "They probably could have run rat races in that time slot and people would've tuned in." But the show was a solid, if not a bit of a one joke pony show, and earned those ratings. The problem was never the show itself, but rather the public's reaction to the show. Angry phone calls and letters from both sides. Jewish people decrying the show demeaned their religion. Which considering how some of the Jewish characters were shown as mere stereotypes, maybe they were right in these criticisms. Catholics were also saying the show demeaned their religion. And then just your ordinary average everyday bigots saying that inter-faith marriages were abominations. The studio even had bomb threats. A premise that would seem uneventful in these modern, more progressive days (well, at least somewhat more progressive) could not cut it in 1972 America, and thus CBS, because of fear of what might happen, did not offer *Bridget Loves Bernie* their well deserved second season.

As a post note, Baxter really did love Birney, and the two were married in 1974. The couple were married all throughout Meredith Baxter-Birney's successful run as Elyse Keaton on the 1980's situation comedy *Family Ties*, before divorcing in 1989. Baxter-Birney, now back to Baxter, came out as a lesbian in 2009, and has since spoken of the physical and emotional abuse she suffered at the hands of her ex-husband. Birney has denied these allegations. Today, although it was a hit in it's day, and is currently available on DVD (unlike the M.I.A. statuses of most of the shows in this book), and can be viewed as a spiritual precursor of sorts to the ABC sitcom *Dharma & Greg* that ran for 5 seasons from 1997 to 2002, *Bridget Loves Bernie*, aside from it's aforementioned unfortunate entry in the record books, is mostly forgotten. Bridget may have loved Bernie, and vice versa, but the powers that be certainly did not love either one.

The Paul Lynde Show (1972-73)

When it aired on ABC for its one and only season in 1972-73, many critics called *The Paul Lynde Show* derivative of CBS's hit show *All in the Family*, but such a thing really wasn't true, as the premise of the show had already been around for more than a decade by this time. It began life as a play called *Howie* in 1961, about a straight-laced lawyer who's daughter marries a brilliant but unmotivated beatnik. Then, in 1962, Paul Lynde brought it to television. Well, he almost brought it to television, in the form of a pilot for CBS. A pilot that was never picked up. Cut to a decade later, and the hit ABC series, *Bewitched*.

Producer William Asher and star and wife Elizabeth Montgomery were contractually bound by ABC and Screen Gems, for a ninth season of *Bewitched*, but with their impending divorce, neither one wished to do said ninth season. So, in order to fulfill their contractual obligations, Asher went back to 1962, and decided to remake *Howie*. ABC agreed, and production went in to effect immediately. And conveniently enough, Asher had the original star of *Howie*, Paul Lynde, right there on the set of *Bewitched*, where he had played the recurring role of Samantha's wisecracking warlock uncle Arthur. Lynde had been campaigning for his own show for a while, and when the opportunity to redo *Howie* popped up, he leapt at it. The show was recommissioned as *The Paul Lynde Show*, and the pilot episode would be an almost identical cover of the aforementioned unsold 1962 pilot. And thus, *The Paul Lynde Show* was born. Unfortunately for Lynde and Asher, the show only lasted one season before being cancelled due to low ratings.

These low ratings, and its eventual cancellation, were probably inevitable, as the show was scheduled against *The Carol Burnett Show* on CBS, and *Adam-12* on NBC, both top 20 hits. But there was more than just bad scheduling that hurt the show. ABC hurt it as well. As I stated in my opening salvo, many critics claimed this was merely a cheap copy of *All in the Family*, the number one rated show on television at the time. Yes, the show and its premise had been around for more than a decade, but such a claim was pretty much on the nose, and in fact, that is exactly how Asher and ABC sold the show. A conservative dad whose daughter marries a lay-about, know-it-all hippie. The problem was ABC though. The network's standards and practices would not allow the cutting edge and controversial subjects that made *All in the Family* such a success over on the seemingly more liberal minded CBS. Lynde had tried on several occasions to talk the network into letting them explore these avenues, but he was met with a stern no every single time. As that was the case, instead of competing with *All in the Family*, the show ended up looking exactly like what it was - a cheap imitation of *All in the Family*. But this was only one of the show's problems.

The other big problem was Lynde himself. First off, Lynde insisted that he get all the jokes and punchlines, leaving his supporting cast as mere cardboard straight men for Lynde's over-the-top antics. Paul Lynde, who was great on *Bewitched*, and quite hilarious as the famed center square on the classic game show, *Hollywood Squares*, has always been one of those comics who were great in small doses, but who became rather annoying in longer stretches. Longer stretches such as starring in a half hour sitcom, week in and week out. Perhaps if he had allowed others in the cast to participate in the humor, instead of being his bland sounding boards, this would not have been as big a factor as it had been. But then again, Paul Lynde could never act the straight man, in any and every sense of the word.

Back in the 1950's, the supposed halcyon early days of television, as well as during the golden age of movies in the 1930's and 1940's, homosexuality was not an open subject. Coming out could have destroyed your career. This being the case, many gay and lesbian actors, were forced to play straight in public. Actors like Cary Grant, Montgomery Clift, Claudette Colbert, Greta Garbo, Joan Crawford, Rock Hudson, just to name a few, were always straight as an arrow when seen in public, ofttimes even taking on fake marriages to hide their real lives. Even into the more freewheeling 70's, this forced hiding of an actor's homosexuality, was a necessary evil. *The Paul Lynde Show* came on the air three years after the riots at Stonewall, but still the gay community was unable to be open about themselves. At least as far as celebrities with careers went. Lynde was one of those in unfortunate hiding. Looking back on his mannerisms today, it is pretty obvious that the man was gay – and didn't really try to hide it. He was nearly as flamboyant as Rip Taylor or even Liberace, but I suppose we were just supposed to ignore this, and believe that he was a straight man, a conservative Middle American yokel. Otherwise, his career would have been affected. This was a sad but all too true reality of the day. But that aside, the show just wasn't all that funny. Lynde was a comic genius in many ways, but one would never know it by watching this show – not that many were watching anyway.

Wait Till Your Father Gets Home (1972-74)

In 1960 ABC premiered *The Flintstones*, the first prime time animated situation comedy ever. It ran for six seasons, and later was a constant in syndication. In 1989, Fox debuted *The Simpsons*, which (as of the writing of this book) 31 years later is still going strong on network TV. In between, only one other animated sitcom lasted for more than one season on the prime time network schedule. No, that show was not the *Jetsons*, which surprisingly lasted just one season in 1962-63. That one multi-season animated prime time show was *Wait Till Your Father Gets Home*, which aired for 3 seasons in syndicated prime time. And ya know what? It was actually a damn good show.

Created by Hanna-Barbera, the same people that had brought us both *The Flintstones* and *The Jetsons*, this new show was a whole hell of a lot more adult oriented than either. Just like *The*

Flintstones had been based on *The Honeymooners*, *Wait Till Your Father Gets Home* was based on the much more subversive *All in the Family*. All the producers on TV at the time seemed to have wanted to cash in on the success of *All in the Family* (see the show which immediately precedes this one). But even with this *All in the Family*-esque take, there was also something a bit more wholesome, a bit more whimsical, a bit more *Happy Days* about this new show. Which worked out perfectly, as Tom Bosley, the patriarch of the Cunningham household in the 1950's set *Happy Days*, voiced the title character of Harry Boyle.

The premise was simple, and familiar if you watched *All in the Family*. Harry Boyle was a conservative businessman who had to deal with a hippie son (voiced by the voice of *H.R. Pufnstuf* himself, Lennie Weinrib), a sexually liberated daughter (voiced by Kristina Holland), a smart ass younger son (voiced by both Willie Aames and Jackie Earle Haley), and a clueless Edith Bunker-esque wife, voiced by Joan Gerber, who did the voice of Freddy the Flute on the aforementioned *H.R. Pufnstuf*. The show was smart and savvy with most episodes revolving around topics that most likely made the censors cringe in their tightly wound panties. Subject matter that was certainly not typical of animated television – even of the prime time variety.

The show, just like the aforementioned *Happy Days*, was a spinoff of the sexually provocative comedic anthology show, *Love, American Style* (see a few chapters back), stemming from the segment titled "Love and the Old-Fashioned Father." A live action pilot featuring Van Johnson was produced, but never shown. This is one of the shows in this book that it is a shame it is not still known and remembered. A funny, well written show, that will hopefully become known again once you all go out and check it out. So go ahead and do that. I'll wait here.

Emergency! (1972-77)

Even though this hit NBC action adventure show about the exciting lives of Los Angeles paramedics, firefighters, and emergency room personnel originally ran every Saturday night at 8:00 from 1972 to 1977, it was in its late afternoon second run syndication spot where this author fell in love. I remember every weekday after school, watching this show right after reruns of *Batman* and *Hogan's Heroes* and just before *Star Trek*. To this late 1970's tween, it was one of the most exiting shows on the so-called boob tube at the time.

The show was created by Jack Webb (of *Dragnet* fame), Robert Cinader (who co-created *Adam-12* with Webb), and Harold Jack

Bloom (one time Oscar nominee for Best Screenplay for Anthony Mann's *The Naked Spur*), with Bloom dropping out after the series pilot. *Emergency!*, or *Emergency One!*, as it has sometimes been referred to, was the story of the Squad 51 paramedics working with the Los Angeles County Fire Department and the emergency room doctors and nurses of Rampart General Hospital. Randolph Mantooth and Kevin Tighe starred as the EMS duo of Squad 51. Robert Fuller, and the husband and wife acting team of Bobby Troupe and Julie London, starred as the ER personnel of Rampart.

Just like what the gritty *Adam-12* did for police when it hit the airwaves in 1968, *Emergency!* made the daily heroics of paramedics more accessible to the general public. At the time of the January 15, 1972 *Emergency!* premiere, there were only 12 paramedic programs in the entire United States, two of which were in the Los Angeles area, thanks to then Governor Ronald Reagan and his 1970 Wedworth-Townsend Act which allowed for the still untested paramedic programs to be trialed in the state. Up until this point, most ambulance personnel were merely glorified first aid administrators. Webb and Cinander wanted the show to be as realistic as could be, and used actual cases from fire department log books. Pioneering EMS leader James O. Page served as technical advisor, and both Mantooth and Tighe were put through rigorous paramedic training for their parts.

More than just an exciting show for tweens and teens and adults alike, *Emergency!* was responsible for bringing the realities of paramedics to the forefront, and in turn, for bringing about laws and standards of practice to expand the programs into the life-saving heroics we see today. For some reason though, no matter how groundbreaking and how important and influential this show was in both it's on screen inspiring of pretty much every rescue show to come after it, and in it's proactive real life applications toward the rapid growth of first responders, it is pretty much forgotten today.

The Shazam!/Isis Hour (1974-77)

Technically, this CBS Saturday morning live action superhero show was two shows in one. The first of these shows was *Shazam*, was based on the DC Comics character also known as Captain Marvel, originally created by by C.C. Beck & Bill Parker for Fawcett Comics in 1939 and sold to DC in 1972, where a law suit from Marvel Comics forced the name change to Shazam. The show began on September 7, 1974. A year later, *Isis*, retitled *The Secrets of Isis* when it hit syndication, joined as a companion series, evolving into the dual titled *The Shazam!/Isis Hour*. After the series' were combined, DC Comics adopted the character of Isis into the mainstream DC continuity, whrre she flounders to this day, am underused and unfulfilled super hero.

Shazam! was the story of teenager Billy Batson, who when saying the magic word of Shazam, would transform into the superhero Captain Marvel. Shazam, for those so interested, was an acronym for the six immortal elders from whose power Captain Marvel was created. These elders were Solomon, Hercules, Atlas, Zeus, Achilles, and Mercury. The teenage Billy Batson was portrayed by Michael Gray, who at the time was best known (and I use that term very very very loosely) as Jeff, the one time (read as one episode) boyfriend of Marcia Brady on a 1973 episode of *The Brady Bunch*. Meanwhile, over on *Isis*, Joanna Cameron, best known at the time (and again, very very

very loosely) as the actress who almost beat out Ali McGraw for the lead in *Love Story*, played mild mannered schoolteacher Andrea Thomas, who could transform into the goddess Isis when trouble arose. Cameron once claimed to have starred in more commercials than any other actor in television history. Whether this bold statement at advertising proliferation was true or not, one groundbreaking thing about the actress' portrayal of Isis is definitely true. By predating *The Bionic Woman* by four months and *Wonder Woman* by seven, *Isis* was the first weekly American live action TV series featuring a female superhero as the lead.

Both shows were produced by Filmation, the production company responsible for tons of sci-fi, fantasy, superhero, and adventure series', both animated and live action, including, but not even close to limited to, *Fantastic Voyage, Journey to the Center of the Earth, The New Adventures of Superman*, and *The Star Trek Animated Series*. The show ran for three seasons on CBS, with the final season airing only a handful of episodes before ending in October of 1976. Both shows, would go onto second run syndication, often as separate entities, but still remain largely forgotten, especially when compared to other fondly remembered comic book shows of the day such as *The Incredible Hulk* or the aforementioned *Wonder Woman*. *The Shazam!/Isis Hour*, or either of the parts of it's sum, is probably even less remembered than the barely remembered live action *Spider-Man* TV series of the day, which incidentally, due to this latter show's difficult to remember status, may be talked about in the inevitable second volume of this book. Foreshadowing galore.

Partridge Family 2200 AD (1974-75)
The Fonz and the Happy Days Gang (1980-81)
Gilligan's Planet (1982-83)

Throughout the 1970's and 1980's, there were a slew and a half of animated versions of hit live action shows, from *Mork & Mindy* to *The Brady Kids* to *Laverne & Shirley in the Army*. There were animated versions of everything from *Star Trek* to *I Dream of Jeannie* to *Punky Brewster*, Heck, there was even a *Roseanne* cartoon at one point. But three of the most intriguing ones, at least to me, were a pair of CBS series' and an ABC series, based on the classic sitcoms, *The Partridge Family*, *Gilligan's Island*, and *Happy Days*, respectively. And all three took on a science fiction bent.

The first to see the light of day was *Partridge Family 2200 AD*. Debuting on the CBS Saturday morning line-up on September 7, 1974 and running for sixteen episodes until March 8, 1975, the show was created and produced by the folks over at Hanna-Barbera. Originally Hanna-Barbera had wanted to do an updated version of *The Jetsons*, with a teenage Elroy and a grown Judy, now working as am ace reporter, but Fred Silverman, head of CBS at the time, discarded the idea and chose to go with an animated version of *The Partridge Family* instead. An animated Partridge Family had already appeared in several episodes of *Goober and the Ghost Chasers*, a Hanna-Barbera series from the previous season – but this new show still had a decidedly *Jetsons* vibe to it.

In this new iteration of the series, The Partridge Family is, without any explanation whatsoever, living the high life in a Jetsons-esque future world of 2200 AD, where they are the musical toast of the galaxy. Along with the regular fam, the show also included Danny's robotic dog named Orbit, as well as a half green half blue flying Martian named Marion, and Veenie, a purple-haired Venusian, who acted as BFFs for teens Keith and Laurie. The show, who's look, from spaceships to spaceports to space outfits to the retro artistic design amidst a futuristic skyline, was so much like *The Jetsons* that there would have been a lawsuit if the two shows had not been made by the same company. We did get a multicoloured Mondrian spaceship, reminiscent of the Partridge bus, but otherwise, it was all pure Jetsons-esque animated production design.

Debuting a few months after the original sitcom's four season run on ABC had ended, only a few of the live action show's cast had come aboard for the family's futuristic space adventures. Danny Bonaduce, Suzanne Crough, and Brian Forster voiced their respective characters of Danny, Tracy, and Chris, but the rest of the original family was notoriously absent. Yes, Susan Dey did voice Laurie in the first two episodes, but was quickly replaced by former *Mouseketeer* Sherry Alberoni for the remaining fourteen. Meanwhile, David Cassidy's Keith was voiced by Chuck McLenan, and Shirley Jones' matriarch was voiced by Joan Gerber, the woman who voiced Freddie the Flute in the Sid & Marty Krofft show, *H.R. Pufnstuf* (see also *Wait Until Your Father Gets Home*). Former Monkee drummer, Mickey Dolenz also did various voices throughout the series – which would be the start of a very productive post-*Monkees* voice over career. The show was retitled *The Partridge Family in Outer Space* when episodes were serialized as part of the *Fred Flintstone and Friends* series in 1977 and 1978. In 2005, two restored episodes were included as bonus material in *The Partridge Family: The Complete First Season* DVD set, but otherwise the series was all but forgotten lo these many years.

The next of this trio of animated sci-fi adaptations to hit the small screen would be *The Fonz and the Happy Days Gang*. This ABC Saturday morning cartoon series ran for 24 episodes over two seasons from 1980 to 1981, and like *The Partridge Family 2200 AD*, was produced by Hanna-Barbera. Based, obviously, on the hit 1950's set ABC series, *Happy Days*, this cartoon, unlike *The Partridge Family 2200 AD*, which aired after it's live action mother was cancelled, ran concurrently with the live action sitcom's 7th and 8th seasons, out of its eventual eleven. The intro of the show was voiced by DJ extraordinaire, Wolfman Jack, which gave it even more of a 1950's vibe, but the 1950's would not be where this series was heading.

The series focused on Arthur "The Fonz" Fonzarelli, Richie Cunningham, and Ralph Malph, all voiced by their original live action counterparts, Henry Winkler, Ron Howard, and Donny Most, respectively. These three were joined by an anthropomorphic dog named Mr. Cool (of course), and a time traveling teenager named Cupcake, voiced by Didi Conn. Cupcake and her malfunctioning time machine would take our intrepid 1950's heroes throughout all of time, from the distant past to the far future. This lost in time motif would be the gist of the entire 24 episode run. We never do see the gang make it back to their beloved 1957, but we do see Fonzie and Mr. Cool join the cast of the animated *Laverne & Shirley in the Army* in 1981, which changed it's name to *Laverne & Shirley with the Fonz* in 1982, and in 1983 would be incorporated into the syndicated animated series *Mork & Mindy/Laverne & Shirley/Fonz Hour*. Even with some episodes found on Youtube, none of these shows are remembered much today.

Next, for 13 episodes in 1982, came *Gilligan's Planet*. Based, again quite obviously, on the CBS situation comedy, *Gilligan's Island*, which ran for three seasons from 1964 to 1967, was actually the second attempt at an animated version of the infamous castaways. The first series, which ran on ABC Saturday mornings for 24 episodes between 1974 and 1977, was a straight up animated rendition of the original series, called *The New Adventures of Gilligan*. This second series though, produced by Filmation, as was the first series, would take our beloved castaways far away from the island. Far far away.

To be honest, the series really wasn't that far away. Yes, it was set far far away, but not in its narrative. The premise was that the Professor managed to build a spaceship to get them off the island. This was probably a bit of overkill, but one supposes the castaways were beyond frustrated and just wanted a way off the island. Any way off the island. So, that is exactly what happened. The castaways shot off in the professor's newly built rocket. Of course they went directly to a distant planet (again, why?) and promptly crash landed, and became stranded once again, this time on another planet. The unluckiest seven bastards on Earth...and now off Earth as well.

All of the original cast returned to voice their respective characters, save for Tina Louise, who had wanted to distance herself from the role of Ginger Grant. Louise had not returned for *The New Adventures* either. To do their own distancing, and possible preemptive lawsuit wrangling, production company Filmation had swapped Ginger from the redhead Louise had been in the original live action sitcom, to a platinum blonde. Filmation had done the same in the aforementioned *New Adventures* too. Dawn Wells, who was unable to do *The New Adventures* due to another project, returned here to voice both her own Mary Ann Summers, and Ginger as well. Of course, just like the previous animated forgotten shows in this chapter, the seven castaways did get a new friend in the form of an alien named Bumper. Bumper was voiced by Lou Scheimer, one of the founders of Filmation.

As mentioned in my opening salvo, these three animated sci-fi spin-offs, were just three of many an animated take-off on a live action hit series of the day. There were animated versions of *My Favorite Martian*, *The Dukes of Hazzard*, and *ALF*. There was even a canine cartoon version of *M*A*S*H*, called *M*U*S*H*, and a bizzaro mash-up of Marlo Thomas' *That Girl* and Alice in Wonderland. Any of these, with the possible exception of *Star Trek*, mentioned earlier, could be included in this book. These just seemed like the most fun to write about. Perhaps we'll discuss some of these other shows in the inevitable sequel to this book.

Holmes & Yoyo (1976-77)
Future Cop (1976-78)

In 1976, eleven years before the film *RoboCop* ever hit screens, but also at the height of fame for *The Six Million Dollar Man* and *The Bionic Woman*, ABC television had not one, but two different shows about robotic police officers. Both of these new robotic shows, one an action/drama, the other a situation comedy, had a lot in common. Other than both being about a down-to-Earth cop buddied with an android cop, both shows were actually quite terrible. Terribly terrible even. Then again, neither one was really around long enough for it matter much.

The action cop show, *Future Cop*, was the first to bow, as its pilot episode aired in May of 1976. Technically this was a made-for-TV movie, but wound up acting as the pilot for the eventual series. However, it was the comedic (well, supposedly comedic) *Holmes & Yoyo*, that got a regular gig first. It debuted in September of 1976, and ran for 11 episodes before being cancelled right before the Christmas TV break. *Future Cop* would finally make it back to television in the Spring of 1977, but for only six episodes before getting itself cancelled as well. Meanwhile, *Holmes & Yoyo* came back briefly in August of that year, with two final episodes that never got a chance to air during its original run. Then, in March of 1978, NBC attempted to re-pilot *Future Cop* as a TV movie called *Cops and Robin*, wherein our human/robot cop partners are assigned to protect a little girl. This time though, it was not picked up to be a series, and fell, pretty much immediately, into obscurity.

Future Cop was the story of veteran cop Joe Cleaver, played by veteran actor, and Oscar winner Ernest Borgnine, who is teamed up with android cop John Haven, played by Michael J. Shannon, an actor mostly known for playing US Presidents on stage and screen (Lincoln once, Warren G. Harding once, and JFK thrice). Meanwhile, over at *Holmes & Yoyo*, we get accident prone cop Alexander Holmes, played by Richard B. Shull. Holmes repeatedly got his partners injured through his own ineptitude, so the department partnered him up with their new android cop, Gregory "Yoyo" Yoyonovich, played by John Schuck. The ineptitude kept happening, but at least now Holmes' new super durable partner would no longer get injured because of said ineptitude.

Holmes & Yoyo was produced by Leonard Stern, one of the producers of the classic sitcom *Get Smart*, as well as one of the co-creators of Mad Libs (seriously!). Stern billed the show as the revival of the classic two-man comedy team. The producer said of the show, "For over thirty years we had the marvelous antics of Laurel & Hardy, Abbott & Costello, Hope & Crosby, Martin & Lewis, Gleason & Carney, and then suddenly came an unexplainable gap. But now, hopefully, Schuck & Shull will fill the comedy void." But alas, considering most of you have probably never heard of Schuck or Shull, let alone Schuck & Shull, Stern's premonition never did come to fruition. Meanwhile, over on *Future Cop*, there was a plagiarism lawsuit, which they lost, and that aforementioned 1978 retooling of the show. Nowadays, these shows are all but forgotten – which is a good thing they are in this book.

Battle of the Network Stars (1976-88)

Gabe Kaplan. Robert Conrad. Dick Van Patten. Lynda Carter. Scott Baio. Kristy McNichol. Billy Crystal. Melissa Gilbert. Ed Asner. Morgan Fairchild. Tom Wopat. Jan Smithers. Lou Ferrigno. Penny Marshall. Greg Evigan. Charlene Tilton. Robert Urich. Valerie Bertinelli. Willie Aames. Gil Gerard. Ann Jillian. Tom Selleck. Gregory Harrison. Diana Canova. Robert Hays.

Bruce Boxleitner. William Sanderson. John Davidson. Erin Gray. Barbara Mandrell. Tim Reid. Joan Van Ark. Nancy McKeon. William Shatner. Jill Whelan. Lorenzo Llamas. Heather Locklear. Randi Oakes. Cheryl Tiegs. Jimmie Walker. Adrien Zmed. McLean Stevenson. Mr. T. And that's just a small portion of this show's "cast."

Actually, *Battle of the Network Stars* was less a show and more a sporting event. A star studded sporting event. Beginning in 1976, the show, this star studded sporting event, was, just as the title more than suggests, a battle between the three networks of the day, and featuring some of the biggest TV stars of the day. You see, unlike today, where TV viewers have options left and right, both on thousands of TV channels, and on the web, back in these aforementioned days, there were just three options. We had ABC. We had CBS. We had NBC. Okay, we had PBS too, but no one other than boring old men and little kids ever watched that. Back then, there were the three major networks, and beginning in 1976, and twice a year (Spring and Fall, during what was known as sweeps week) every year through 1985, and one more time in 1988, the stars of these three networks would gather together to have their own little Olympic games.

The idea was that each team would consist of 8 to 10 players (it changed throughout the years) with team captains, and they would participate in 8 or so events each year. Changing throughout the years, the events included tennis, a swimming relay, a running relay, a bicycle relay, golf, a frisbee catch, kayak, an obstacle course, touch football, a dunk tank, and even a game of Simon Says. There was a host each games (Howard Cosell hosted or co-hosted 18 of the 19 shows) and a commissioner who was usually a famous athlete of some sort. Points were awarded and after these events, the third place network was kicked to the curb, and the remaining two would compete in a sometimes epic game of tug-o-war for the championship. I say sometimes epic because one of these tug-o-wars actually went on for ten minutes. Another was an easy win for CBS, since they had *The Incredible Hulk* on their network, and the rather massive Lou Ferrigno as their anchor. I think that may have been a bit unfair. These events, though a friendly atmosphere overall (the dunk tank and Simon Says showed a fun camaraderie between the network stars) could also get quite heated at times, especially when you had argumentative seventies tough guy Robert Conrad at the helm of NBC 5 of the first 7 games.

In the first games, on November 13, 1976, *Welcome Back Kotter*'s Gabe Kaplan in the first of his five consecutive turns as the ABC captain pointed out that NBC had cheated in the relay race. Granted, this was merely a mistake on one of their runners parts, but it didn't stop the network from being disqualified and having the win given to Kaplan's team. This also didn't stop the cocksure (and quite obnoxious) NBC captain Bob Conrad from pitching a hissy fit, and crying that it was unfair because it wasn't anyone purposely cheating. Finally, the frustrated (and frustrating) Conrad challenged Kaplan to a one-on-one 100 foot race to determine the winner. After the brash tough guy Conrad, who played the balls-to-the-wall US Marine Major on *Baa Baa Black Sheep*, and who at the time had a battery commercial daring someone to knock the battery off his shoulder, was beaten by a rather embarrassing mile by the not very athletic looking stand-up comic turned sitcom star Gabe Kaplan, ABC would go on to win the whole kit and caboodle that year.

These silly temper tantrums aside, this star studded sporting event always looked like fun time had by all. Well, maybe not Conrad, but everyone else seemed to be having a blast. Rewatching these old shows while preparing this book, it does seem a bit antiquated in it's rather sexist take on women, seen as mere sex objects at the time, but *Family* star Kristy McNichol toppled that stereotype by being one of the best athletes at the games, male or female. McNichol set a record, then broke it the following year, on the obstacle course. Generally though, the stars seemed to be having a blast, and some of these stars, like the aforementioned McNichol, were great athletes to boot. Billy Crystal, who was on ABC's *Soap* at the time, even set a touchdown record in 1978. And this wasn't just an event with B and C list stars in it. Yes, there were many of those, but the show also had some of the biggest names in TV at the time. Ron Howard. Suzanne Somers. Tom Selleck. Daniel J. Travanti was the NBC team captain right after winning his second straight Outstanding Actor Emmy for *Hill Street Blues*.

Circus of the Stars, where celebrities (Loni Anderson, Scott Baio, Bob Barker, Dixie Carter, Downtown Julie Brown, and even Lauren Bacall, among many many others) performed circus-type acts, was a similar show that ran concurrently with *Battle of the Network Stars* – but that's another story for another book. In the end, ABC, which also broadcast all 19 editions, won the most, with 7 victories. CBS and NBC each had 6 wins. In 2017, ABC brought the show back as a weekly series featuring battles between sitcom stars vs. cop shows and TV sex symbols vs. variety show hosts and so on and so on. This later series included mostly newer stars, but they did sprinkle in a few of the so-called old-timers, like Greg Evigan, Ted Lange, Catherine Bach, and Willie Aames. This latest iteration was not near as fun as the older shows. Sadly, this show, that made this author so happy when he was but a wee lad, has like all the other shows herein, been mostly forgotten.

Blansky's Beauties (1977)
Who's Watching the Kids? (1978)

There are genuine spinoffs, with genuine characters spinning off into their own shows (*The Jeffersons, Rhoda, Frasier*) and there are what one calls backdoor spinoffs, where characters are introduced for a single episode (or two) for the express purpose of spinning them off into their own shows (*Mork & Mindy, Empty Nest, NCIS*), and then there are these two shows, ostensibly spun off from *Happy Days*, but you would never know it from watching them – not that anyone ever did.

It all began on the February 12, 1977 episode of the hit ABC series, *Happy Days*, when Howard Cunningham's cousin Nancy Blansky, came to visit for his and Marion's anniversary. In reality, cousin Nancy, played by Nancy Walker, currently on a hiatus from her Emmy nominated role of Ida Morgenstern on CBS's hit series *Rhoda*, came to visit in order to get herself spun off onto Garry Marshall's second spinoff of the creator's ABC hit *Happy Days*. Eight nights later, *Bansky's Beauties* premiered on ABC. Inconsistencies became obvious right away. Even though it's *Happy Days* back door pilot took place in or around 1957, the story of *Blansky's Beauties* is set in the, then contemporary, year of 1977, with Nancy Walker's Nancy Blansky looking pretty much the same as she had twenty years earlier. This was made even more ridiculous with the addition of former *Happy Days* cast members Roz Kelly reprising her Pinky Tuscadero role, and after the cancellation of his short-lived sitcom, *Mr. T and Tina*, Pat Morita, reprising his Arnold role – both looking pretty much identical to how they looked in 1957, save for Pinky's more contemporary shag haircut. I guess stars were more ageless back in the day.

The show itself was set in Las Vegas, and revolved around a group of showgirls managed by Ms. Blansky. These showgirls shared Nancy's apartment, as did her nephews Joey and Anthony DeLuca. To further tighten the ties between shows, Joey was the younger cousin of Carmine "The Big Ragoo" Ragusa, from the most successful of all *Happy Days* spinoffs, *Laverne & Shirley*. He was played by Eddie Mekka, the same actor who played the aforementioned Big Ragoo. At least here he was supposed to be the younger cousin, so the age disparity was a bit more realistic. The rest of the cast consisted of Lynda Goodfriend as bubble headed Sunshine, Rhonda Bates as tall lanky spitfire Arkansas, a young Scott Baio as leering 12 year old ("going on 28") Anthony, and Caren Kaye, basically acting as second lead to Walker, as Bambi Benton, the one with both brains and beauty. The show lasted 13 episodes, with it ending on June 27, 1977. And after rewatching these 13 episodes in preparation for this book, one wonders how it lasted even that long.

After the cancellation, Garry Marshall took two of the show's cast members and integrated them into his *Happy Days* setting. Lynda Goodfriend came on as Lori Beth Allen, love interest and later wife to Ron Howard's Richie Cunningham, while Scott Baio was added as Charles "Chachi" Arcola, young cousin to Henry Winkler's Arthur Fonzarelli. A few seasons later Pat Morita would move back to Milwaukee to reprise his role of diner owner Arnold, when his replacement on that show, Al Molinaro, left to do yet another *Happy Days* spinoff, *Joanie Loves Chachi*. But Marshall wasn't quite done with Blansky's Beauties yet.

In 1978, Marshall created a new pilot called *Legs*, which took pretty much the crux of *Blansky's Beauties* (aka, all the pretty showgirls), switched some names around, and tossed it into a brand new show, this time for rival network NBC. Out were Walker and Mekka, both going back full time to *Rhoda* and *Laverne & Shirley*, respectively. In were Caren Kaye, now known as Stacy Turner, as well as the newest members of the *Happy Days* gang, Lynda Goodfriend as Angie Vitola, and Scott Baio as her 15 year old brother (he aged three years in less than a season) Frankie Vitola – both doing double duty on their respective shows. The show would get picked up by NBC, and with a name change to *Who's Watching the Kids?*, and a more "family friendly" set-up (less on the leggy dancers and more on the family situations of the girls and their younger wards), and with the addition of Tammy Lauren as Stacy's 9 year old kid sister Melissa, and Larry Breeding and Jim Belushi as the sitcom trope of the hapless neighbors, debuted in September 1978. This show lasted just nine episodes (+ 6 unaired) and ended in December 1978.

With the inevitable cancellation of Marshall's second attempt at this same story, Goodfriend and Baio would go back to their full time gigs on *Happy Days*, and make a pretty good career of it as well, especially Baio who would get a short-lived spinoff of his own before starring in the hit CBS series *Charles in Charles* for five seasons from 1984 to 1990, before eventually falling off the quite slippery deep end of right wing politics in more recent times. As for *Blansky's Beauties* and *Who's Watching the Kids?*, they would fall through the cracks of television history to become nothing more than a mere footnote in the history of the much more successful *Happy Days*. One could even say these shows jumped the shark before there was even a shark to jump.

Quark (1977-78)

On May 25, 1977, a film called *Star Wars* would premiere in theatres. Within a few months, the film was the biggest thing ever. With the success of *Star Wars*, film and TV producers went crazy desperately trying to recreate the film's huge success. Everything from the likes of *Battlestar Galactica* to Disney's *The Black Hole*, copies trying to cash in on the success of *Star Wars* seemed to be the only things getting produced in Hollywood at the time. The funny thing about NBC's *Quark*, a show that seemed to be yet another one of those cheap copies, is that it was not a copy at all. In fact it's pilot episode hit airwaves more than two weeks BEFORE *Star Wars* debuted in theatres. Maybe creator Buck Henry was even more ahead of his time than we thought. Or maybe, instead of making a cheap knock-off of *Star Wars*, he was actually just making a cheap knock-off of *Star Trek* instead. Which, in watching the show, is exactly what Mr. Henry was doing. Although never truly succeeding in its initial three season run on NBC, *Star Trek* had been given a second life in syndication (which is where this author first fell in love with Gene Roddenberry's baby) and was building in popularity throughout the 1970's, with a series of successful films just around the corner, and even though there were references to *Star Wars* in some later episodes, it was *Star Trek* that was the biggest influence on *Quark*.

As I already stated, *Quark* was the brainchild of Buck Henry, the man who, along with Mel Brooks, had created *Get Smart*, one of the smartest and best situation comedies ever made. Henry went from spy spoof to sci-fi spoof. Sadly, *Quark* does not share in those accolades for *Get Smart*. But more on that in a bit. The show was set on a United Galaxy Sanitation Patrol Cruiser, an interstellar garbage scow operating out of United Galaxies Space Station Perma One in the year 2226. This garbage patrol was captained by Adam Quark, played with deadpan comedic furor by the underrated comedic actor Richard Benjamin. Other garbage ship personnel included Betty I and Betty II, aka, The Bettys, played by identical twins Cyb and Patricia Barnstable. The Bettys were the ship's pilots. One was a clone of the other, but each one thought the other was the clone. Then there was Ficus Pandorata, played by Richard Kelton. Ficus is Quark's Spock-like science officer, and a member of the sentient plant alien species, the Vegetons.

The show also featured Tim Thomerson as Gene/Jean, a Transmute alien being, with full sets of male and female chromosomes. Looking back on the show, this "he/she" character, who fluctuated between macho gung-ho Gene and demure and stereotypically feminine Jean, often within the confines of a single scene, can be seen as rather transphobic in nature. In the less progressive, less self-aware time period of 1977, I don't think Henry or the writers were purposely being transphobic, but just like how the blackface of the 1920's through 1950's in Hollywood, which was the so-called norm at the time, was still quite racist, the gay and gender stereotypes of the 1970's and 1980's were still quite homophobic. But then again, it wasn't this that made *Quark* a failure. The thing that did that was that it just wasn't all that good of a show.

I remember watching this as a space obsessed 10 year old, and loving it. I also remember being upset that it did not last that long. Looking back on the show now, my adult sensibilities can clearly see it was not really all that good after all. Yes, Benjamin was good on the show, as was Conrad Janis as the sleazy bureaucrat who runs Perma One, the year before he was cast on *Mork & Mindy* as Mindy's daddy, and there are a few funny moments throughout, but overall, one wonders how it even lasted as long as it did. And how long did it last? Counting the May 1977 pilot and the seven episodes that ran as a mid-season replacement from February through April 1978, it lasted a whole eight episodes before getting itself cancelled. I suppose, thanks to it's cult following, it isn't quite as forgotten as some of the other shows in this book, but it's not exactly a household name either.

The Man from Atlantis (1977-78)

Before he became the iconic Bobby Ewing on the equally iconic CBS über-soap *Dallas*, the man who could come back from the dead as if it were but a dream, Patrick Duffy was the web-footed hero of the short lived not so iconic NBC series, *Man from Atlantis*. The story of this somewhat laughable sci-fi adventure series, is as simple as the show was simple-minded. Duffy played an amnesiac man rescued from the sea, and thought to be the lone survivor of the great kingdom of Atlantis. Given the name of

Mark Harris and put to work as a secret operative for the government, this man from Atlantis, complete with webbed toes and fingers, the ability to breathe underwater and swim like a dolphin, not to mention having super strength (though I did just mention it), was the hero none of us ever knew we needed. Yeah, it ends up he wasn't really all that needed or wanted at all.

The short-lived show had a supporting cast that consisted of Belinda J. Montgomery (the future mom of *Doogie Howser M.D.*) as Dr. Elizabeth Merrill, the prolific Alan Fudge (who appeared in almost every made for TV *Columbo* movie – and there were quite a few of them) as C.W. Crawford, Jr., and the great Victor Buono (the affable villainous King Tut from the 1960's *Batman* series) as the show's biggest baddie, Mr. Schubert. *Man from Atlantis*, obviously more than somewhat based on some combination of the Marvel Comics character, Namor the Sub-Mariner and DC Comics character Aquaman (who was merely a cheap knockoff of Namor anyway) started out as a series of four TV movies airing on the network in the Spring of 1977. The series proper began on September 22, 1977 and ran for a mere 13 episodes (with a four month hiatus in midseason) before having it's plug pulled and the pool drained at the end of the season.

As for the quality of the show – perhaps the pool should have been drained long before it's thirteenth episode. With special effects by a team lead by Gene Warren, the man who gave us those spectacularly awful, but admittedly kitschy special effects on the Sid & Marty Krofft show *Land of the Lost* (who incidentally had a son who went into the family business and actually won himself an Oscar for the visual effects on *Terminator 2: Judgement Day* – talk about outdoing the generation before you), and the stiffest of acting from Duffy, and a writing team that may have consisted of those proverbial monkeys at a typewriter, *Man from Atlantis* may be one of the blandest shows in this book. Granted, I remember enjoying the show as a ten year old boy, but what ten year old boy wouldn't like a show such as this. Critic Tom Shales, reviewing the show for The Washington Post, said that "kids may be impressed" but the show lacked any "adult appeal" and it would surely "soon wear thinner than water." Looking back, I guess the guy wasn't far off.

Hee Haw Honeys (1978-79)

The classic country music comedy variety show *Hee Haw*, a rural spun alternative to the much hipper pop culture comedy of *Rowen & Martin' Laugh-In*, ran for 26 seasons. The show ran on CBS from 1969 to 1971, then in syndication from 1971 to 1993, and then on TNN in 1996 and 1997. This corny, yet fondly remembered series, which aired 655 episodes over those two and a half decades, is far from forgotten, and therefore has no reason to be spoken of in a book such as this. So, you may be asking yourself, why am I reading about this hit series right now? The answer is quite simple. We are here to briefly discuss the equally brief run of the corny show's even cornier spin-off, *Hee Haw Honeys*.

Running for just 24 episodes, *Hee Haw Honeys* spun off from it's pappy for the 1978-79 TV season, and revolved around the goings-on at Lu-Lu's Truck Stop in *Hee Haw*'s Kornfield County. This show starred Kathie Lee Johnson, the woman who would later be known as Kathie Lee Gifford, and *Hee Haw* regular Misty Rowe, who was one the parent show's bevvy of buxom cornfed babes known as the Hee Haw Honeys, which obviously, is from whence the name of the spin-off derives. Styled after *Hee Haw*, the show was a musical comedy, fluctuating between corny (and often not very funny, and even more often quite sexist) sketches and musical numbers by such country music dignitaries as Loretta Lynn, Barbara Mandrell, Larry Gatlin, The Oak Ridge Boys, and *Hee Haw* hosts Roy Clark & Buck Owens.

The spin-off took the folksy humor of *Hee Haw*, and honed in on the more sexist aspect of it's blatant objectifying of women, which was just one portion of what *Hee Haw* was (and to be fair, no more or less objectifying than *Laugh-In* was), and created a show that was pretty much nothing but. Luckily for all involved, the show was cancelled after one season. Misty Rowe and most of her cohorts were blended back into their parent series, while Kathie Lee went on to her own form of Emmy Award winning super stardom with Regis Philbin. The show itself went spiraling back into oblivion..

Star Wars Holiday Special (1978)

I'm not sure if you've heard of it, but in the Summer of 1977, a little film by the name of *Star Wars* hit theatres. You could say it was a hit. A big hit. The biggest hit. Okay, obviously, unless you've been in a coma for the last 40 years, you know that *Star Wars* became one of the biggest film franchises in cinematic history, and has spawned the second most successful movie franchise of all-time. And it is only the second most successful because of the over proliferation of the Marvel Cinematic Universe's 22 films as compared to the 12 films of *Star Wars*. But I digress. Second or not, it's 9 billion dollar total box office and nearly 300 billion dollar sales in merchandise make it a behemoth of pop culture. The franchise was seemingly foolproof - even godawful mistakes in judgement such as Jar Jar Binks somehow ended up in the success column (sort of). It's as if *Star Wars* could do no wrong. Well, on November 17, 1978, a year and a half after the film's initial release, George Lucas would say to that statement, hold my beer.

It was on this date, at 8pm on CBS, that Lucas gave us *The Star Wars Holiday Special*. It aired one time, and one time only. It has since become known as one of most ridiculous, one of the most heinous, one of the most reviled things to ever appear on a screen, big or small. It also became a cult classic, sought after by any and all *Star Wars* aficionados. A joke, yes…but a highly coveted joke. But this highly coveted joke, this cult classic status, did not start right away. To be honest, this one time TV special was all but forgotten after its original airing. Lucas had not released it on home video. In fact, Lucas would never release this on home video, nor would he allow it being shown by anybody, anywhere, at any time. It's almost as if he's embarrassed by the whole thing. And take it from me, he damn well should be. I mean, the man willingly gave us Jar Jar Binks, and has never tried to hide the fact, but this one shot holiday special is the one and only thing he never wants us to see again. And that was almost the case.

David Hofstede, author of *What Were They Thinking?: The 100 Dumbest Events in Television History*, ranked this holiday special at number one, calling it "the worst two hours of television ever." Nathan Rabin of *The A.V. Club* said of the show, "I'm not convinced the special wasn't ultimately written and directed by a sentient bag of cocaine." These negative reviews could probably take up an entire book by themselves, so I'll leave it at that, which is probably what George Lucas, who later admitted he never really had anything to do with the special even though he reportedly saw daily rushes during filming, would want us all to do. But that was not to be the case. After being pretty much forgotten by all for a decade and a half, this special starting showing up in bootleg copies throughout the *Star Wars* world of fans and collectors in the 1990's. Duplicated from original TV recordings, and then reduplicated over and over again, the video quality of these bootlegs were quite a bit shy of quality, but nonetheless, there they were, and there once again, whether we wanted it or not, was *The Star Wars Holiday Special*. And there it still is today.

As for the special itself, it was the story of Life Day, a Wookiee holiday similar to our Christmas, and the celebration thereof on the Wookiee homeworld of Kashyyk. The special has appearances by Mark Hamill, Carrie Fisher, Harrison Ford, Peter Mayhew, and other original *Star Wars* actors. We also get the pleasure of Bea Arthur as Ackmena, owner of the Mos Eisley Cantina, as well as Harvey Korman, Diahann Carroll, Art Carney, and even the band Jefferson Starship. The special gave us sci-fi adventure, family fun, and (supposed) comedy, as well as musical numbers, which inculed Bea Arthur singing, and a whole array of variety show-esque antics.

The one and only highlight of the special (other than Bea Arthur's singing of course) was a cartoon segment featuring the first ever appearance of the character Boba Fett. This cartoon, written by Lucas himself, has some continuity problems with later storylines (like Han and Boba Fett not knowing ach other), but otherwise, it is the one and only bright spot in this travesty of television, and it is also the only portion of said travesty to ever get an official release from Lucas.

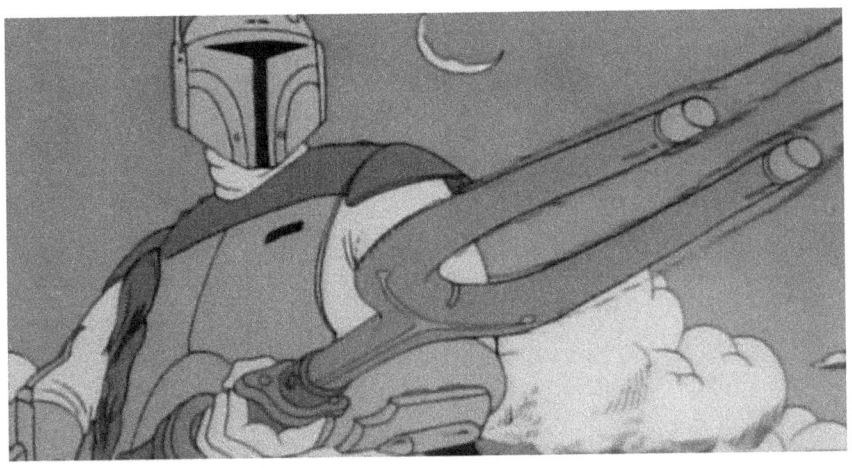

Overall, *The Star Wars Holiday Special* was such a bizarre piece of television and *Star Wars* history, one almost needs to watch it to experience what may be the most gloriously messed up moment in television and *Star Wars* history. From Bea Arthur's song and dance number, which I am positive the actress considered her most embarrassing moment on screen, to Diahanne Carroll's equally embarrassing erotic musical number which plays out as some sort of phone sex fantasy between her and grandpa Wookiee, this thing is both horrifying and splendiferous at the same time. I remember crying as a wee 11 year old, when the stormtroopers destroyed all the Wookiee's Life Day presents. The special ends with a song by Carrie Fisher as Princess Leia. Word has it, that Fisher, Ford, and Hamill only did their respective cameos in the special because of contractual obligations (or maybe blackmail by Lucas), but one might conjecture that Fisher did her part only on the stipulation that she get to sing a song just like dear old mom did in her many musicals at MGM. In the end, thanks to it's cult following, and the fact that it is part of the *Star Wars* Universe, this television train wreck, for better or for much much worse, may never be truly forgotten.

Struck by Lightning (1979)

This long forgotten CBS comedy is the story of Boston high school science teacher Theodore "Ted" Stein, who inherits his late grandfather's creepy old New England inn, which is inhabited by an equally creepy old caretaker named Frank. It turns out that Ted is the real live descendant of the actual Dr. Frankenstein, and Frank is his original monster. Frank convinces (aka threatens) Ted to stay and recreate his ancestor's formula, which Frank needs every fifty years or so, in order to survive. And there you have it. The title derives from Frank being struck by lightning whenever he goes outside. Personally, I think they should have named the show *Frank n Stein*, but that's just me.

The show starred Jeffrey Kramer as Ted Stein. Kramer's claim to fame, for it's worth, was playing Deputy Jeff Hendricks, second in command to Chief Brody in *Jaws*, and again in *Jaws 2*. Our loveable monster was played by legendary character actor Jack Elam. Elam hadn't wanted to take the role at first, due to not wanting to have to sit for hours of make-up each shooting day. Lucky for him, he wouldn't have to. Although he did wear padding to make him look bulkier, and lifts to make him taller, the producers told the actor that, thanks to his bulging eyes and crooked face, he would not need to wear any makeup to play the monster. "I was both pleased and somewhat offended when the producers asked me to play the Frankenstein monster without makeup," the actor explained. "It's not too flattering to play the monster with my normal face, but the money they offered me made up for it."

CBS ordered 11 episodes of *Struck by Lightning*, but after just three, due to low ratings, the network put the show on a hiatus. It would be a hiatus from which the show would never return. The final 8 episodes would never air on US television, although they would eventually see the light of day in both Australia and the UK. Even though it had a promising premise, the show was panned by most critics, save for the performance of Jack Elam. A veteran actor, mostly known for the Western genre, with memorable performances in such films as *Rancho Notorious*, *High Noon*, and *Once Upon a Time in the West*, and on TV's *Gunsmoke*, Elam got raves even amongst the pans for pretty much everything else the show had to offer. Personally, this author agrees with such an assessment. A show that should only be remembered for Elam's hilarious monster. Then again, perhaps if they had named the show *Frank n Stein*, like I said, it might have been a hit. Or perhaps not.

Hello, Larry (1979-80)

After three seasons on the hit CBS series, *M*A*S*H*, McLean Stevenson left his Lt. Col. Henry Blake behind in Korea, to take on bigger and better parts. So determined to end his time on *M*A*S*H*, for which the actor had become frustrated with his third banana role, Stevenson insisted his character be killed off. This sitcom death is still to this day, considered one of the most emotional moments in television history. But alas, for Stevenson's career, it too was nothing short of death itself. While *M*A*S*H* went on for another eight seasons after Stevenson's early departure, garnering over 100 Emmy Award nominations, and is still heralded today as one of the greatest TV shows of all time, Stevenson would go from one failed series to another and another and yet another. Sure, he got to be the lead he had always coveted in all four of these post M*A*S*H sitcoms, but none of them ever came even close to the success of what he had so determinedly left behind.

His first foray into leading man status came with *The McLean Stevenson Show*, which ran for 12 episodes on NBC during the 1976-77 television season. Stevenson played a hardware store owner. In 1978, Stevenson was back on CBS, as a conservative priest opposite a sassy street-wise nun for 9 episodes on *In the Beginning*. In 1979, Stevenson had his biggest success, as a radio talk show host on *Hello, Larry*, which ran for two seasons, and 38 episodes on NBC. Then, in 1983, over at ABC, Stevenson would be a landlord in the series *Condo*, which lasted a whole 13 episodes. All four of these shows, which ran for a combined whopping total of 72 episodes, had their respective runs while *M*A*S*H* was still on the air. One could say his decision back in 1975 never exactly paid off. He did do a few *Love Boat*'s in this time period, as well as appearing in the "hit"

movie, *The Cat from Outer Space*, and even did a *Golden Girls* episode. So I guess he was golden after all. He even managed to squeak in a fifth failed series in 1988, as Baby's father in the CBS TV version of *Dirty Dancing*. Golden indeed.

With its two season run, *Hello, Larry* was the closest thing Stevenson could call a success in his post M*A*S*H life. The show however was, plain and simple, just not that good. It surely wasn't Stevenson's worst show (just take your pick of any of the other three) but it was by no means whatsoever, an actual success. The show started out as a midseason replacement in the 1978-79 season. The basic storyline was Larry, a recently divorced father of two, who moves from L.A. to Portland, to start his and his teenage daughters lives over. At first, *Hello, Larry* was a more adult-oriented comedy, based around Larry's job as a talk radio host, but after it's first few episode's complete and utter failures, the format was changed to a more bumbling but loveable single father comedy, now showing more of the home life than the work life. This change also came with a switch from 9:30 to 8:30.

In this more family oriented timeslot, the show would follow the hit series *Diff'rent Strokes*. In the hopes of raising the ratings of *Hello, Larry*, NBC created a crossover between the two series. It is revealed that Stevenson's Larry Adler had been old war buddies with *Diff'rent Strokes*' Phillip Drummond (Conrad Bain), with Drummond's company buying the station where Larry worked. NBC also added Harlem Globetrotter Meadowlark Lemon to the cast, playing himself, in an attempt to raise viewership. But alas, these new ploys did not work, nor did the ratings ever improve, but NBC did end up renewing the series for the 1979-80 season anyway. Maybe NBC chief Fred Silverman had a soft spot for Stevenson, remembering him from back in his M*A*S*H days, when Silverman ran CBS and first put that show on the air in 1972. Whether that was the case or not, the failure of

Hello, Larry was one of the main things that got Silverman boot as network president.

To be fair, no one is really sure how the show ended up getting a second season renewal, but it did, which made it the now leading actor's best chance at the stardom he once had ahold of on *M*A*S*H*. But again, that never did happen. In truth, Stevenson and *Hello, Larry* became the butt of jokes in Hollywood. Even fellow NBCer, Johnny Carson would regularly lampoon the show on *The Tonight Show*. *Hello, Larry* would become comedy shorthand for what bad TV was all about. In the Spring of 1980, long after it probably should have been, the show was finally cancelled.

The joke didn't stop there though. One critic of the day, created "The Annual McLean Stevenson Memorial 'I'm Gonna Quit This Show and Become a Big Star' Award." In 2002, TV Guide ranked *Hello, Larry* No. 12 on their "50 Worst Shows of All-Time" list. But the critics and comics were not the only ones taking jabs at Stevenson. In 1990, the actor said that leaving *M*A*S*H* was the biggest mistake of his life, stating that "I made the mistake of believing that people were enamored of McLean Stevenson when the person they were enamored of was Henry Blake."

This rather sad tale of TV failure ended on February 15, 1996, when McLean Stevenson shuffled off this mortal coil after a heart attack. In a weird coincidence, the following day, Roger Bowen, the actor who played Henry Blake in the 1970 movie *M*A*S*H* also passed away from a heart attack. I don't know if there is a moral to this story, but it does make for a rather twist ending. Or not. Anyway…Farewell, Goodbye and Amen.

Legends of the Superheroes (1979)

Everyone of a certain age remembers the *Super Friends* on Saturday Morning television. It is an iconic show for many a comic book fan of my generation, or even the generations after me, as it still to this day, plays on Boomerang and Cartoon Network. Based on DC Comics' Justice League of America series, *Super Friends* was a Hanna-Barbera production that ran for sixteen episodes during the 1973-74 season, and then in syndication ad infinitum after that. This hit show was followed by *The All-New Super Friends Hour* in the 1977-78 season. This is the one that introduced the Wonder Twins. Then the following year came *The Challenge of the Super Friends*. This version of the Saturday Morning cartoon was a weekly battle between the Super Friends and the Legion of Doom. This was also the series that made Hanna-Barbera, the undisputed kings of TV animation, decide to spread their wings and try their hands at a live action superhero show. Really guys, you should have stuck with the animation.

Legends of the Superheroes was not a regular show so much as a pair of hour long TV specials, running in consecutive weeks in January of 1979. Produced and directed by long time game show producer Bill Carruthers, these two specials reunite Adam West and Burt Ward as Batman and Robin, for the first time since their series went off the air eleven years prior. Also including Captain Marvel, Green Lantern, The Flash, Hawkman, Black Canary, and others, the first special revolves around the Legion of Doom trapping the Justice League, and an all out battle royale finale. Among the Legion of Doom were Dr. Sivana, Sinestro, The Weather Wizard, Solomon Grundy, and The Riddler, here portrayed once again by Frank Gorshin from the aforementioned 1960's *Batman* series. The second episode is a celebrity roast of the superheroes, hosted by Ed McMahon. This episode also features Ruth Buzzi as Captain Marvel villainess Aunt Minerva, and an African American superhero called Ghetto Man. Yup, you read that correctly.

Overall, the two episode special event was just plain awful. Stilted acting, delivering inane dialogue, with cheap special effects and costumes, even by 1979 standards. As I stated earlier, perhaps William Hanna and Joseph Barbera should have stuck to the animation they did so well. In this day and age of comic book movies and TV shows being the crux of the entertainment world, one could easily look back on live action comic book shows of the 1970's with disdain for their seemingly low production standards. It is true that special effects of the day may seem cheap in comparison to what we are now used to in all of today's *Avengers*-esque glory, but 1970's era shows such as *The Incredible Hulk* and *Shazam* and the like still have a nostalgic charm to them, in much the same way the 1933 *King Kong* does, even with it's obvious archaic visual effects. Sadly, no one can make this claim for the simply godawful mess that was *The Legends of the Superheroes* – quite possibly the worst show in this book.

B.J. and the Bear (1979-81)

If one were to be asked by aliens to describe the 1970's with a single TV show, one would be hard pressed to find a show any more quintessential of that bizarre little decade that could, than that show about a truck driver and his chimpanzee best bud and co-pilot. Seriously, with trucker films and shows pretty much a dime a dozen back in the day (*Smokey and the Bandit*, *Convoy*, the TV series *Movin' On*) and C.W. McCall's 1975 number one smash hit "Convoy," and with the film *Every Which Way but Loose* combining truckers with great apes (in this case Clint Eastwood and an Orangutan named Clyde), there is probably not a more archetypical 1970's TV show to show to those aforementioned aliens. But what about the show itself? Let's discuss that, shall we?

The show was created and produced by Glen A. Larson, the man who had already created *Alias Smith and Jones*, *The Hardy Boys/Nancy Drew Mysteries*, and *Battlestar Galactica*, and would go on to create *Buck Rogers in the 25th Century*, *The Fall Guy*, *Magnum P.I.*, and *Knight Rider*. It starred Greg Evigan as Billie Joe "B.J." McKay a long haul independent trucker who rode around the country in his red & white Kenworth K-100 semi, with his chimpanzee Bear, named after former Alabama head coach Paul "Bear" Bryant, and solved crimes and saved beautiful damsels in distress. All with a smile on his face, a song in his heart, and a gleaming wink in his eye. Evigan quickly became a magazine cover boy and the hottest hunk on TV.

But it wasn't just Evigan. It was the show as a whole. *B.J. and the Bear* was an instant hit for NBC when it debuted as a midseason in 1979. So much so, that after just six episodes, Claude Akins, who had played B.J.'s not so honest (but not totally corrupt) law enforcement nemesis, Sheriff Elroy P. Lobo (the Smokey to Evigan's Bandit) was spun off into his own show, quaintly titled *The Misadventures of Sheriff Lobo*. Ratings did not stay high though, but *B.J. and the Bear* did still manage to last for three seasons (or two and a half since it was a midseason replacement) while *Lobo*, which the spinoff's title was shortened to for it's second season, lasted for two, both ending their run in May of 1981. The show was quintessential 1970's, but that wore thin once the 1980's hit.

Several old-timers such as John Carradine, Edd "Kookie" Byrnes, Slim Pickens, and Harry Carey Jr., made appearances on the show, as did soon to be big names like Danny Glover, Ted Danson, and even Andre the Giant. Evigan, who had done musical theater prior to B.J. (most notably on Broadway as Danny Zuko in *Grease*), would go on to star as one of the two titular dads in NBC's *My Two Dads*, before having runs on *Melrose Place* and the daytime drama, *General Hospital*. Nowadays though? Other than for novelty's sake, does anyone remember this series? Yes, *B.J. and the Bear* is probably better known and remembered than some of the shows in this book, but I wouldn't exactly call it a fondly remembered hit.

Real People (1979-83)
That's Incredible (1980-84)

In the tradition of *You Asked for It*, which ran on Dumont and later ABC, from 1950 to 1959, and showcased non celebrities (aka, the real people) doing daring and strange things, came a pair of reality shows for the early eighties. A pair of shows that highlighted the real, but also the strange and interesting, the bizarre and awe-inspiring, the cool and the downright freaky. The first of these shows to debut was NBC's *Real People*, on April 18, 1979. Next up came *That's Incredible*, premiering nearly a year later on ABC, on March 3, 1980. Both shows lasted for five seasons, ending in 1984 and 1985, respectively.

Real People was executive produced by George Schlatter, the creator of *Rowen & Martin's Laugh-In*, and was hosted by Sarah Purcell, John Barbour, Byron Allen, Fred Willard, Bill Rafferty, and Skip Stephenson. *That's Incredible* was created and produced by Alan Landsburg Productions, who had already given us the crypto-mystery series *In Search of...*, and would later produce

Gimme a Break! and *Kate & Allie*, and was hosted by John Davidson, Cathy Lee Crosby, and Fran Tarkenton. With the exception of comic genius Fred Willard, who was already a name from *Fernwood 2 Night*, *That's Incredible* definitely had the bigger name hosts. Davidson was already a name due to his hundred plus appearances on Hollywood Squares - a show he would later host himself. NFL Hall of Famer Tarkenton spent nearly two decades as the quarterback of the Minnesota Vikings, and Crosby, who was a former tennis star and actress, holds the distinction of being the first person to portray Wonder Woman on TV, in a 1974 made for TV movie, more than a year before Lynda Carter began her series.

Both shows were similar in their approach, though *That's Incredible* was definitely more death defying. While *Real People* showcased mostly quirky stories of people with strange hobbies or out of the ordinary occupations, *That's Incredible* had people doing stunts and illusions. Some stunts were so dangerous that many called the show irresponsible, and ABC had to place "do not attempt this at home" disclaimers before some of their riskier segments. One of the non death defying moments on *That's Incredible* was when US Army Lt. Col. Earl Woods brought his five year old son Eldrick in to show off his incredible golfing skills. Little Eldrick would eventually grow up, change his first name to Tiger, and do a bit of professional golfing himself. You may have heard of him.

Both shows were ratings hits at first, consistently in the top twenty, but both fell off in their fifth and final seasons. In 1980, *Real People* spawned two very short-lived spinoffs, *Speak Up, America* and *Real Kids*. The latter was hosted by kiddie commercial icon, Messy Marvin, aka Peter Billingsley, who would join the cast of *Real People* after his show ended. Billingsley would also go on to star in the perennial Christmas favourite, *A Christmas Story*. Also in 1980, *Those Amazing Animals* would spinoff of *That's Incredible*, as an animal centric take on the show, hosted by Burgess Meredith, Priscilla Presley, and Jim Stafford. There was also an attempted revival of the show in 1988, called *Incredible Sunday*, hosted by Davidson, fashion model Cristina Ferarre, and Tracey Gold of *Growing Pains*. Today, even though the reality TV series is a full blown (and quite overblown) genre, these two forerunners are not all that well remembered. Now if only we could get people to forget about all the other reality shows out there, the world might be a better place.

Pink Lady & Jeff (1980)

This 1980 variety show is a strange creature, indeed. It could actually be the strangest of all the variety shows. Not the dumbest or the worst, mind you. After all, *The Brady Bunch Hour* does exist. But *Pink Lady and Jeff* is very possibly the strangest of 'em all. The premise of the thing is thus: *Pink Lady* (the show only became known as *Pink Lady and Jeff* in retrospective) was a show hosted by Japanese pop singing duo Pink Lady, made up of Misuyo Nemoto and Keiko Masuda, and the very very whitebread American comic, Jeff Altman. Yup, this show, which lasted just five episodes during the Spring of 1980 (a sixth episode was filmed but never aired), took a flash-in-the-pan Japanese pop sensation (really, these girls were the next big thing for about a minute-and-a-half), neither of whom knew more than a handful of English words to string together, and teamed them up with an equally unknown stand-up comic, whose biggest claim to fame was playing a sleazy record producer in the movie *American Hot Wax*, two years prior. Whatever could go wrong?

The whole shebang was the supposed brainchild of TV exec-cum-miracle worker, Fred Silverman. Silverman was kind of a TV guru back in the day. He was the TV exec responsible for putting some of the best shows on television. With a slew of successes at both CBS (*All in the Family, The Mary Tyler Moore Show, M*A*S*H, Barnaby Jones, Kojak*, the Saturday morning cartoon, *Scooby-Doo Where Are You?*, as well as the revival of *Match Game*) and ABC (*The Love Boat, Fantasy Island, Charlie's Angels, Soap, Three's Company*, the morning show *Good Morning America*, the mini-series *Roots*, as well as bringing *Scooby-Doo* over from CBS with him) already under his belt, Silverman came to NBC, as President and CEO in 1978. But it wouldn't be all wine and roses for Silverman at the Peacock Network. With several high profile failures like *Hello Larry* (see a few chapters back) and *Supertrain*, as well as that first Lorne Michael-less season of *Saturday Night Live*, Silverman handed the world *Pink Lady*, in all its absurdity.

Granted, there would be music and comedy sketches and guest stars and all the typical variety show jazz. The strange thing is that it was a kitschy Japanese pop duo and some seemingly random generic white guy. One of the running gags of the show was the aforementioned inability of either Pink Lady to speak English, other than in cutesy-pie broken style, and the oh so easy jokes that come from such a trite and obvious gag. Though the ladies did sing their songs in English, through memorization of the lyrics, it was surely a whole hell of a lot sexier to have them giggle and say cute, funny things. The fact that they were often put in provocative clothing, sure didn't hurt. Silverman had already been known for bringing what was often called "Jiggle TV" to ABC, with shows like *Charlie's Angels, Three's*

Company, Love Boat, and other shows with scantily clad women, and it was obvious that the NBC president was trying to repeat that at his new network. But alas, after just five episodes, Pink Lady was ripped from the line-up. Yes, Silverman did have hits at NBC. Shows such as *Diff'rent Strokes, Facts of Life,* and *Hill Street Blues,* as well as being the guy who gave David Letterman his first network TV gig, but he would not last long enough to bask in the glory. But enough about Fred Silverman. Let's talk more about this forgotten show.

The show itself was produced by Sid and Marty Krofft, the minds behind such classic cheezy kid's programming as *H.R. Pufnstuf, Lidsville, Dr. Shrinker,* and *Land of the Lost.* Any red-blooded American kid growing up in the early 1970's, as did I, will fondly remember these and many more from their childhood. And as with their aforementioned *Brady Bunch Hour* variety show (yeah, the Kroffts were behind that one too), the final result was just a big ole steaming pile of weird. Sometimes this brotherly duo would hit gold with their weird shows (I loved the inherent weird in most of the old Krofft shows) but in the case of *Pink Lady,* or *Pink Lady and Jeff,* if you will, the weird just didn't work. And the talked about in-fighting probably did not help either.

Supposedly, the reason the show was simply called *Pink Lady* on screen was due to Pink Lady's management threatening a lawsuit if Altman's name was in the title. Even though it was Altman who actually carried the show, his name was kept off the title card. Then again, in most advertising, the show was listed as *Pink Lady and Jeff.* Perhaps they figured the ladies read English as well as they spoke it. Who knows? Either way, the show is mostly forgotten today. But I must admit, I actually do remember this show rather fondly, even if the rest of you don't. I mean, I like weird, so it worked for me.

True, it only aired five times, but the show did have a slew of famous guest stars. Granted, these big-name celebrities had to be coerced by even bigger paychecks. Guest stars on the show included the likes of Roy Orbison, Sid Ceasar, Jerry Lewis, Florence Henderson, Bobby Vinton, and even Donny Osmond, whose show, with sister Marie, was also produced by the Krofft Brothers - all paid extremely well in order to agree to appear on a dying genre like the variety show of 1980.

The show also showed videos by the likes of Blondie, Cheap Trick, and Krofft pal Alice Cooper, back at a time when videos were still a very, very new thing. The show also boasted an appearance by Hugh Hefner and several of his adoring playmates. I figure Heff fit in perfectly with Silverman's attempt at bringing back his "Jiggle TV." After all, at the end of each show, the Kroffts would dress up their star ladies in string bikinis, and the bikini-clad Pink Ladies would then pull co-host Jeff Altman, tuxedo-clad himself, into the on stage hot tub. This was sort of their thing. Maybe that's the reason Hugh Hefner did the show. I know my thirteen year old self sure enjoyed it, and perhaps this is why I haven't forgotten the show like the rest of you have.

Inside Story with Slim Goodbody (1980)

A tall skinny guy with a white guy afro, clad in a skin tight body suit, covered in painted-on muscles and bones and internal organs galore, singing to kids about the inner workings of the human body while doing not so groovy dance moves and the occasional cartwheel, the whole time going by the name of Slim Goodbody? How could this not be the greatest television show ever? Created by John Burstein while working at a New York hospital in 1974, as a way to entertain sick children, the character of Slim

Goodbody was more than just a guy on what had to be the greatest television show ever. Much much more.

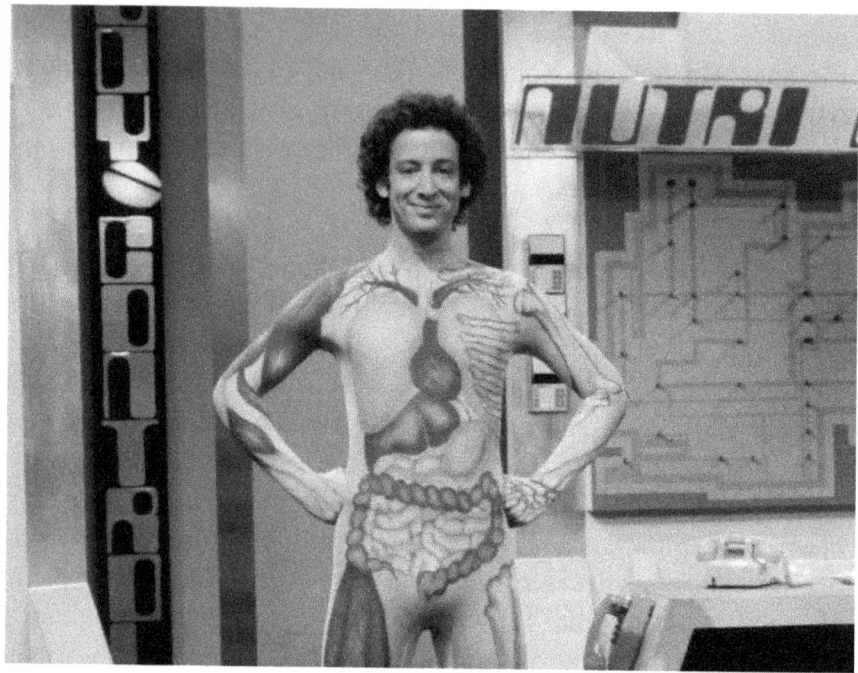

In 1975, Burstein took his Slim Goodbody character outside the hospital, and became a sensation on the children show circuit. Slim found himself making appearances on both *The Today Show* and *Good Morning America*, and between 1976 and 1981, he would appear twice a week on the daily kids program, *Captain Kangaroo*, becoming somewhat of a household name in nutrition and anatomy and general health and hygiene merriment. It was while being part of Captain Kangaroo's regular cast of performers, that Slim Goodbody, and by obvious extension, John Burstein, managed to win his own show on PBS.

This show was called *Inside Story with Slim Goodbody*, and ran for a year on PBS. Kids would learn all about the human body through Burstein's elaborate song and dance numbers. Slim's former buddy, Captain Kangaroo also made a few appearances. After *Inside Story*, Slim found himself doing show after show after show all throughout the 1980's and 1990's and he is still doing it today. From short films to commercials to a Nickelodeon show – even an appearance on a Radio Shack commercial during the 2014 Superbowl – Slim Goodbody has kept busy entertaining children with his unique blend of vaudeville and science. He never became as famous a kids performer as that stupid purple dinosaur or those creepy Wiggles guys, but he has kept going all these years. You should check him out online. Trust me, it's worth the look. It wasn't just hyperbole when I asked how could this not be the greatest television show ever?

Fridays (1980-82)

On Saturday, October 11, 1975, at 11:30 pm, a new kind of show debuted on NBC. It was called *NBC's Saturday Night*, later to be changed to *Saturday Night Live*. You may have heard of it. This show was the breeding ground for dozens upon dozens of big name comedy stars. From John Belushi and Chevy Chase to Bill Murray and Eddie Murphy, to Mike Myers, Will Ferrell, Tina Fey, Amy Poehler, Jimmy Fallon, and a slew of others, *Saturday Night Live*, has always (well, almost always) been the place to be for any aspiring comic actor. As of the writing of this book, *Saturday Night Live*, or *SNL* as all the cool kids call it, is enjoying its 45th season on the air. I'd say that is rather an impressive run. Of course, since everyone and their grandmother has heard of *Saturday Night Live*, this is not the show we are here to talk about in this chapter of Forgotten TV. We are here to talk about another sketch comedy show, a copycat sketch comedy show, but a copycat show that may have, at times, been better than *SNL*. Yeah, so there.

It was in the Spring of 1980, as *SNL* was in the middle of its fifth season as the late night king, that ABC had finally decided to take the plunge, and challenge NBC and their hit late night sketch comedy show. Granted, this new challenge would not be a head to head battle. I mean, come on, the good folks at the good old Alphabet Network were brave, but they weren't stupid. So on Friday (not Saturday), April 11, 1980, they debuted their new sketch comedy show at 11:30 pm. It was brilliantly titled, *Fridays*, and it was immediately met with the harshest of criticisms. Most critics called it nothing more than a mere *Saturday Night Live* wannabe. And of course, in many ways, that is exactly what *Fridays* was. Featuring sketches and musical acts, even a news segment, just like *SNL*, *Fridays* was a blatant rip-off of *Saturday Night Live*. But really, what sketch comedy show isn't a blatant rip-off of *SNL*? Granted, *Fridays* was not the first copycat show, nor was it the last, not by a long shot, but unlike many of these so-called wannabe doppelgänger shows, this was actually a quality show, even if the critics did not see that during its brief, 12 episode first season.

But then something happened over at *SNL*, something that would affect how critics looked at *Fridays*. Sometime between the first and second season of *Fridays*, and the fifth and sixth seasons of *SNL*, the entire playing field changed. Well, at least the late night sketch comedy playing field. After a somewhat mediocre fifth season (the show had lost both John Belushi and Dan Aykroyd to movie careers, and the remaining cast was riddled with drug and personal problems) *SNL* creator, Lorne Michaels decided to jump ship, and the entire staff (writers and actors both) jumped with their beloved commander-in-chief. This brought in a new, untested showrunner in Jean Doumanian, and a new cast and crew of writers that just weren't all that funny. With the lone exception of breakout Eddie Murphy, who entered the show more than a month after the season began, and would not be a regular cast member until later on in the year, this new cast was a dud, and the critics saw this. Suddenly, many of the same people who called *Fridays*, a cheap imitation of *SNL*, during its opening season, were now calling the show an edgier, smarter version of the now quite lackluster *Saturday Night*. Nothing had changed at *Fridays*. The show was no more or less edgy or smart in its second season, than it had been in its first, but now the competition was no longer all that dangerous or daunting.

But enough about what the critics liked. Let's talk about the show itself. As I said, it was set up a lot like *SNL*, though set in Los Angeles as opposed to *SNL*'s New York setting. But, just like *SNL*, the cast was made up of relative unknowns. At least unknown outside of the stand-up and improv circles of the day. Most of these cast members would never be heard from again, or at least not in any substantial way. Two of the cast members however, would become well known. Along with names such as Mark Blankfield, Brendis Kemp, Bruce Mahler, and Melanie Chartoff, the *Fridays* cast also included both Larry David and Michael Richards. David, of course, would go onto co-create and write the smash hit sitcom *Seinfeld* (one of the best shows of all-time), which co-starred fellow *Friday* alum, Michael Richards, as the always entertaining Cosmo Kramer. David would later create and star in a comedy of his own, *Curb Your Enthusiasm*. Both Chartoff and Mahler would also make appearances on *Seinfeld* throughout its nine season run, as did David himself, most notably as the voice of George Steinbrenner. But back in 1980, David and Richards were still unknown improv players, and had to prove themselves on the live stage of late night sketch comedy.

Many, if not most of the *Fridays* sketches were political in nature, taking on the then newly elected President Ronald Reagan, the so-called Moral Majority, gun control, the Middle East, the wars in Central America, and even evolution versus creationism. But even with this overtly socio-political bent, it was an innocent-seeming sketch about a young happy couple eating in a zombie diner, that got the show kicked off of several local ABC affiliates. In just the third episode of the first season, there aired a sketch titled "Diner of the Living Dead," where a road-weary couple enter a diner that is populated by the sitting dead, all munching down on such delicacies as heart salad, toe stew, and the belly burger. Tame by today's standards, many in the prudish set, apparently thought it gross and/or offensive, and after complaints came filtering in, several affiliates stopped carrying *Fridays*. Combine this with the critical drubbing the show received early on, and it is actually a wonder the show ever saw a second season. But it did see a second season, and a third one, and with the aforementioned downward spiral of the folks over at NBC's *Saturday Night*, the show actually became a hit, albeit a mild hit, but a hit nonetheless.

Actually there were a lot of different sketches worth noting, and a lot of different characters too. Due to the show being mostly forgotten after all this time, none of these characters have had the lasting appeal of many of the more famous *SNL* characters (Eddie Murphy's Gumby or Mr. Robinson; Mile Myers' Wayne Campbell; Kristen Wiig's Target Lady – just to name a very few), but there are still a few who deserve mention here. One is Mark Blankfield's pharmacy owner, who is a frantic mess, popping every pill he can find (he even drinks the liquid from a pregnancy test in one sketch). The more intriguing character was one created and performed by Michael Richards. His name was Dick, a pompous, clueless fool, who thought he was god's gift to pretty much everything. Watching this recurring character, probably the most popular one on the show, one can easily see the embryo, or even the pupa stage, of the creature that would eventually metamorphose into Jerry Seinfeld's wacky neighbor. The most famous sketch on the show though, came in season two. It was a satire of *Rocky Horror*, called "The Ronnie Horror Show." With song and dance numbers that parodied the new right wing white house, and complete with cast member John Roarke playing Ronald Reagan in full-on Tim Curry drag, the sketch opened the show, ran for nearly twenty minutes, and received a standing ovation at the end. Imagine that.

But alas, things could not go well forever. Well okay, *Saturday Night Live* may be celebrating 45+ years on the air (not all good though), but *Fridays* would only last three. During those three seasons, *Fridays* was a big proponent of the new wave music movement that was taking over the early 1980's music scene. Much more than *SNL*, *Fridays* had many new wave and post-punk acts on their show. From Devo and The Clash to The Plasmatics and The Tubes, the scene at *Fridays* was much hipper than the one over on Saturday nights. So hip in fact, that Dick Ebersol, executive producer of *SNL* in 1982, made an offer to the entire cast to jump ship and come over to his show. This offer was met with a unanimous no, though both David and cast mate Rich Hall did briefly join the *SNL* cast in 1984, two years after *Fridays* left the air. And speaking of leaving the air, *Fridays* did sit high for a while but when ABC decided to expand *Nightline* to five nights a week at 11:30, *Fridays* was shoved back to midnight, and its viewership dropped drastically. In one final attempt to save the show from cancellation, ABC decided to place the show in its primetime schedule. The only problem was that they placed it opposite CBS's top rated drama, *Dallas*. After just one primetime episode, *Fridays* was canceled. Today, some random highlights can be found in a highly incomplete DVD set from Shout Factory, and some others can be found online, but as with most of the shows in this book, *Fridays* is sadly (and wrongly) forgotten.

It's a Living (1980-82, 1985-89)

On October 30, 1980, at 9:30 pm, nestled between already established shows *Barney Miller* and *20/20*, ABC premiered a brand new situation comedy. It was called *It's a Living*. It was not a hit. It was a smart and funny show though, and should have been a hit. But alas, it was not. The show was about five waitresses working at a restaurant on the top floor of the Bonaventure Hotel in Los Angeles. There really is a restaurant on the top floor of the actual Bonaventure Hotel in Los Angeles, but I am guessing Ann Jillian never worked there. These waitresses consisted of the sensible married mother of two Lois (Susan

Sullivan), flighty actress Dot (Gail Edwards), the virginal small town girl Vicki (Wendy Schaal), single mom and overworked full time college student Jan (Barrie Youngfellow), and blonde bombshell sassy Cassie (Ann Jillian). The show also featured hard-nosed boss Nancy (Marian Mercer), temperamental chef Mario (Bert Remsen), and sleazy piano player Sonny Mann (Paul Kreppel).

The main crux of the show were these five main women trying to live their lives as best they could. The show was full of what, at the time, was seen as risqué situations and even more risqué language. Frank and honest talk about sexuality that would seem tame by today's standards, but on prime time TV in 1980, was bad enough to earn the ire of many a moral majority type organization. Similar to the moralistic furor over the soap opera satire sitcom *Soap*, when it premiered in 1977 (on the same network), and was starting it's fourth and final season in 1980, *It's a Living* was called immoral by many a conservative critic. Unlike *Soap* though, which did well in the ratings, *It's a Living*

would barely make it to a second season due to this backlash. But it did make it through, but not without some major retooling.

For the 1981-82 season ABC changed the name of the show to *Making a Living*. Maybe they thought this name change would fool the self-righteous naysayers. Who knows? That crowd isn't known for their smarts. Anyhoo, this name change was not the only change the show had coming. Just like the name, three of it's cast were kicked to the curb as well. Susan Sullivan, who was the top-billed star of season one, Wendy Schaal, and Bert Remsen all got their pink slips that summer between seasons. Sullivan would go on to star in *Falcon Crest* on CBS for the next nine years, before becoming Kitty Montgomery on *Dharma & Greg* for five seasons back on ABC. Wendy Schaal, after a one season stint as Hervé Villechaize's replacement on the hit ABC series *Fantasy Island*, would delve into movies in the 1980's, including *Inner Space*, *The 'Burbs*, and *Small Soldiers*. Today Schaal is best known as the voice of Francine Smith on Fox's animated hit *American Dad!*, which, as of the writing of this book, is preparing for its 18th season on the air. Remsen meanwhile, went back to the character roles he was already known for in movies.

In this new iteration, we were given a new chef (Earl Boen) and a new waitress in Louise Lasser playing Maggie, a lovable bubblehead not that far removed from her title character on the soap opera satire *Mary Hartman, Mary Hartman* from 1976-77. The show stayed just as snarky and sassy, and just as smartly written and performed as the first season, but alas, the people were still not watching, and the show was cancelled after two seasons on ABC. Even though this would be the end of the line for *Making a Living*, this would not be the end of the line for *It's a Living*. In 1983, all 27 episodes went into syndication, and the ratings went through the roof. Well, as far as a syndicated show's ratings could go through any roof. This surprise turnaround in popularity, along with the stardom of Ann Jillian, who was definitely the breakout star of the series, and who had just been nominated for both an Emmy and a Golden Globe for her portrayal of Mae West in a television movie, prompted the show's producers to try and bring the show back to television. Jillian's new sitcom, *Jennifer Slept Here*, a modern take on *The Ghost & Mrs. Muir*, was a flop, so she was willing to come back, so in 1985 a third season of the show, back to its original title, began airing in first run syndication.

For this third season, Lasser was gone and replaced by Crystal Bernard, who had just come off of a 16 episode run as K.C. Cunningham on the penultimate season of *Happy Days*. The rest of the ladies were back though. It girl Ann Jillian, who now got top billing, as well as both of the other original waitresses, Barrie Youngfellow, and Gail Edwards, who coincidentally had been offered the role of K.C. Cunningham on *Happy Days*, but missed out when her agent turned down the role without her knowledge. Also back were Mercer as boss lady Nancy and Kreppel as obnoxious Sonny Mann. There was also Richard Stahl replacing Boen as head chef. These two actors looked so much alike that I don't even know if the audience noticed or not. *It's a Living* managed to do something in its first run syndication that it could never do on ABC. Become a hit. But that didn't stop Jillian from leaving after season three to concentrate on her recovery from breast cancer, with which she had been diagnosed shortly before the show went into first run syndication. The show went on without her though. Season four brought on Sheryl Lee Ralph to round out the waitress staff. Youngfellow would now get top billing. Although it was not as good without Jillian, the show ran for four seasons in syndication (six overall) and ended on April 8, 1989.

Gail Edwards would go on to have recurring roles on both *Blossom* (as Six's mother) and *Full House* (as Danny Tanner's one time love interest), before retiring from acting in 1994. She made a one episode comeback in 2017, for the rebooted *Fuller House*. Paul Kreppel kept working steadily, best known for his role as Jackie's dad on *That 70's Show*. Bernard would go on to co-star in the inexplicably popular sitcom *Wings*, which lasted for an excruciating 8 seasons on NBC. Stahl would go onto many supporting film roles before passing away in 2006. Marian Mercer would also go onto multiple roles on television, herself passing away in 2011. Youngfellow retired from acting in 1998. Ann Jillian beat cancer and would go on to star as herself in the 1988 made-for-TV movie, *The Ann Jillian Story*, which chronicled her battle with cancer. She would receive her third Emmy nomination for this film, and would win the Golden Globe for Best Actress in a Mini-Series or Motion Picture Made for TV. Jillian also got her own self-titled sitcom for a season in 1989-90. Semi-retired, she now works as a motivational speaker in California. A smart and sassy show, highlighted by the smart and sassy Ann Jillian, that should not be forgotten.

Best of the West (1981-82)

When I was but a bratty thirteen year old TV addict 8n the Summer of 1980, I decided I wanted to run my own network. With this in mind, I sat down with notebook in hand, and created enough shows to fill a Fall TV schedule. I had sitcoms and dramas, action shows and soap operas, sci-fi shows and cop shows and variety shows, and anything else my budding teenage mind could conjure up. Somewhere down the line, these notebooks went the way of many childhood memories, lost somewhere in time. Though mostly forgotten thirty plus years later, there is still one show that holds court in my fading memory banks. That show was a sitcom I called *Daniel Boom*. What can I say, I was a thirteen year old kid. This show was set in the old west, and was about an inept small town sheriff. Now I'm not saying that ABC stole my idea for their 1981 show, *Best of the West*, but it is rather curious that a year after I came up with my old west sitcom, the alphabet network debuted their own. But alas, let's let bygones be bygones, and move on with our lives.

Seriously though, *Best of the West*, which was one of those myriad of one season wonders from back in the day, was actually a damn fine show. When I was doing research for this book, I thought perhaps it was just some sort of nostalgic hindsight that made me remember the show so fondly, even if it was a blatant rip-off of my own show. But I digress. Not too bitter, huh? To prove to myself that this all-but-forgotten show was indeed as good as I remembered it to be, I went back and binge-watched the entire 22 episode run. I really did want my memories to be right, and I was not disappointed. The show was wryly funny, with deft comic timing, and a cast that always kept the comedy going, without ever having to resort to cheap laughs or silly over-the-top antics. This was something that was rather rare in the early 1980's TV world, and looking back from my still TV-obsessed modern day vantage point, I am actually quite surprised ABC did not renew this show for a second season. The show sat between *Mork and Mindy* and *Barney Miller* on Thursday nights, both successful shows, Granted, it did go up against *Magnum P.I.* on CBS, but still, its ratings could not have been so bad as to warrant having its plug pulled after just one measly season.

Set around 1870, the show starred Joel Higgins, the year before he would star in the moderate hit, *Silver Spoons*, one of those aforementioned early 1980's shows full of cheap laughs and silly, over-the-top antics. Higgins played Sam Best, a Civil War veteran and widower, who decided to head west after the war, and start a new life with his son, and his new bride, played by Meeno Peluce and Carlene Watkins, respectively. When arriving in Copper Creek, expecting to be just the proprietor of the general store, Sam finds himself becoming the town sheriff. The show also featured Tony Award Winner (and Academy Award nominee for *Fiddler on the Roof*) Leonard Frey as Parker Tillman, the man who thought he owned the town. There was also prolific character actor Tracey Walter as Frog, Tillman's inept henchman, and the legendary Tom Ewell as the town drunk.

Guest starring in three episodes, including the pilot, Christopher Lloyd played the perplexing recurring character, a gunslinger known as the Calico Kid. This would have been during the fifth and final season of *Taxi*, a show which aired later in the same evening as *Best of the West*, so Lloyd's character of Reverend Jim on that ABC show, was already well established. You can see more than a few traces of Reverend Jim in his Calico Kid, as Lloyd stole each and every moment of his three episodes. Sadly, neither Lloyd nor anything else in this highly underrated comedy could save it from the executioner's axe at the end of season one. Maybe it's a good thing though. I mean, if it had gone on to be a big hit, I would have had to sue, and that would not have been pretty. Lots of paperwork and all that.

Square Pegs (1982-83)

A generation before she would become Carrie Bradshaw, some might even say the veritable voice of said generation, on HBO's *Sex and the City*, Sarah Jessica Parker would be nerdy, four-eyed freshman Patty Greene, in CBS's one season and done sitcom, *Square Pegs*. Unlike the previous season, full of duds and a bunch of one-and-done shows, where *The Fall Guy* and *TJ Hooker* were the biggest new shows of the season, the 1982-83 television season was one chock full of new hit shows - hit shows galore even. From the strictly mainstream popularity of silly yet popular shows like *The A-Team* and *Knight Rider,* to the more critically acclaimed fare such as *Family Ties, Remington Steele,* and *St. Elsewhere,* to the comeback of Bob Newhart in the simply titled *Newhart,* the new Fall season was the best one in several years. And then there's the wonderfully kitschy and deftly sardonic *Square Pegs*. Whatever became of this oh so overlooked gem-in-hiding?

In the last chapter, I stated that *Best of the West* was easily the best new show of the 1981-82 season, and was unjustly dismissed and canceled without having the chance to catch on with the right audience, an audience that may have propelled it into the hit it should have been. Well, *Square Pegs* was just as unjustly dismissed and canceled before it too could land its rightful audience, and become the hit it should have become. As for it being the best new show of its season, that mantle has probably been stolen away by another sitcom, NBC's *Cheers*, which actually performed dismally in the ratings (74th out of 77 shows), and was lucky that someone at the network was behind it enough to give it a second season, where it would move into TV history as one of the best sitcoms of all-time, even spawning a spin-off which would become even more successful in its own right. So where was that love for *Square Pegs*, I ask you? Where was that love? This was yet another show (this book is chock full of 'em) that was much better than its short history would lead you to believe.

Created by SNL alum, and former National Lampoon writer, Anne Beatts, and based on her own high school experiences, *Square Pegs* was the story of two best friends trying their damnedest to fit into the often socially traumatizing world of being a high school freshman. In the pilot episode, we meet the eight freshmen who will be the stars of the show's strong, albeit quite short run. This cast of eclectic characters is led by the intelligent but awkward Patty Greene, Anne Beatts' on screen doppelganger, played by the aforementioned miss Parker, and her chubby, braces-laden BFF, Lauren Hutchinson, played by Amy Linker, wearing a fat suit to chub the normally thin actress up a bit. The show would follow these two hapless wouldbe social climbers as they try to make their way through the typical trials and tribulations of high school.

The rest of these girls' eclectic band of misfit classmates are filled out by nerdy wannabe stand-up comedian Marshall Blechtman (John Femia) and Johnny Slash (Merritt Butrick), the soft-spoken New Waver, with the ubiquitous shades and walkman. The popular kids were comprised of the quintessential bitchy Valley Girl, Jennifer DiNuccio (Tracy Nelson, daughter of sitcom and music legend, Ricky Nelson), her lunkhead boyfriend, Vinnie (John Caliri), and Jennifer's best friend LaDonna (Claudette Wells), the sole minority character in the cast. The eighth member of the ensemble is the annoyingly peppy preppy, Muffy Tepperman, played by Jami Gertz, future star of just about every teen film of the 1980's.

Granted, the show did have a few plot holes that were never explained, the biggest of which was the apparent age of some of these supposedly 14 year olds. Even though these kids are meant to be high school freshman, both Johnny and Vinnie are shown driving in various episodes, which means they are at least sixteen year old freshmen. Such a blatant gaffe can be explained though. Well, sort of explained. In the pilot episode, we are told that Johnny has been held back, and Vinnie is the dumb one of the bunch, so it makes sense he was held back as well. This may be stretching reality a bit but if one suspends one's disbelief, one can move on to the rest of the show. And considering how many shows and films of the day used adults to play teens (just look at the age of the cast of *Grease*), it is kind of refreshing to see a cast of mostly actual teenage actors playing teenage characters - even if the ages of said characters are a bit in question.

And speaking of said young cast, they were made up of a bunch of unknown teen actors, most of whom ranged from 16 to 19 in age. Some of these actors would go onto virtual obscurity in the showbiz world (Amy Linker has since gotten a degree in French Studies, and is now a teacher) but a few would go onto bigger careers in the biz. As was already stated in our opening salvo, nerdy outcast Patty Greene was played by Sarah Jessica Parker, who would go onto a movie and TV career that would garner her both box office fame and a few Emmy Awards to boot. Both Nelson and Gertz would also go onto bigger things as well. Gertz would costar in such films as *The Lost Boys* and *Less Than Zero*, and would later appear in the TV series, *Still Standing*. Ozzie and Harriet's granddaughter would later star opposite Tom Bosley as a crime-solving nun in *Father Dowling Mysteries*. Meanwhile, Merritt Butrick, who at 23 was the elder statesman of the cast, would get the opportunity to play Captain Kirk's son in both *Star Trek II: The Wrath of Khan* and *Star Trek III: The Search for Spock*. Sadly, a few years later, Butrick would die at 29, due to complications from AIDS.

The show also featured guests stars such as Tony Dow, of *Leave it to Beaver* fame, playing Patty's little seen dad, as well as several of Beatts' old *SNL* pals, like Don Novello in his Father Guido Sarducci guise, and Bill Murray, already the star of *Meatballs* and *Stripes* by this point, as the best substitute teacher anyone could ever ask for. And we were given guest musicians as well. In the pilot, New Wave band The Waitresses, performed the show's title song, which would be turned into the theme song of the show beginning with the second episode. Oddly, this title track would shuffle back and forth in future episodes, with the Chopsticks-esque track that played in the pilot.

And even though *Square Pegs* never lasted as long as its material deserved to last, the show was an influence on the teen films of John Hughes. One can see the influence of Beatts' portrayal of high school angst and its lovable loserdom in such films as *Sixteen Candles, The Breakfast Club*, and *Pretty in Pink*. The cult status and uniquely realistic language of the show also can be seen in Judd Apatow's *Freaks and Geeks*, a 1999 show, but a show set just two years prior to *Square Pegs*. The show may not have been a hit, but someone was watching - someone other than just me - and that can be seen in many a teen comedy and/or drama that has come along the highway ever since. Everything from *Saved by the Bell* to *My So-called Life*. And all this without any seeming love when the show was originally on. And what of this love?

A few paragraphs back, I had wondered aloud about the seeming lack of love for *Square Pegs*. Well, there was some love, for sure. The show actually started off rather well. Taking the 8pm Monday slot that used to be occupied by *M*A*S*H*, which CBS had moved to 9:00 for the show's final season, *Square Pegs* won good ratings for its first few weeks on the air, before steadily declining over the rest of its run. The show also received mostly good reviews from the critics of the day. Cramming the show with hot contemporary references ranging from Pac Man to Monty Python to a slew of fresh New Wave bands such as The B-52's and Devo, the latter of which appeared and performed in an episode, Beatts made the show hip and stylish for all those fellow high schoolers of the day.

I know that my own love for the show came from my being pretty much the same age as the characters on the show (I was a sophomore to their freshmen) and also my love of the New Wave music so loved by Johnny Slash, the character my fifteen year old self most aspired to be, complete with my own braided rat tail. That's right! But the show's hip style, and youth culture bent, though it was still highly influential, was not enough to save it from the executioner's inevitable axe.

But still, it may not have been weak ratings (still higher than those for *Cheers*) nor any sort of alienation of the so-called older crowd sitting at home on their collective couches, that caused this witty show to wave bye-bye to primetime. According to most sources, the demise of the show came from the inexperience of those writing, directing, and producing it. Beatts and her cohorts may have had talent when it came to the creative side of things, but when it came to actually running the show, these relative kids, many not all that much older than their teenage stars, were well in over their heads. There were also rumors about rampant drug use behind the scenes, possibly another crossover from Beatts days at *Saturday Night Live*, but such rumors have never been confirmed by any one associated with the show, so mere rumors they must stay. But alas, whatever the reason for the show's demise, it is still a shame that we never got to see Patty and Lauren and the rest of the gang, graduate high school. Maybe we would have even seen Johnny finally graduate as well. It's totally a loss...totally.

Bring 'em Back Alive (1982-83)
Tales of the Gold Monkey (1982-83)

In the fall of 1982, to cash in on the box office success of *Raiders of the Lost Ark* the year before, both ABC and CBS decided to get in on the swashbuckling hero biz. Both networks hired strapping young bucks to do their own rough and tumble version of Harrison Ford's Indiana Jones. Both networks set up shows around these actors that would highlight their adventurous charm and derring-do. Both networks were hoping to be the small screen home of a copycat of one of the most popular movie characters of the day. Both networks failed. The first of these copycat series to arrive, on September 22, 1982, on ABC, was *Tales of the Gold Monkey*. Two nights later *Bring 'Em Back Alive* would arrive on CBS. By season's end, both shows were gone.

ABC's *Tales of the Gold Monkey*, as much inspired by films such as *Casablanca*, *To Have and Have Not*, and especially *Only Angels Have Wings*, as it was by *Raiders of the Lost Ark*, was the story of pilot Jake Cutter, and his adventures as a smuggler in the South Pacific in 1938. The show starred Stephen Collins, three years after captaining the USS Enterprise in *Star Trek: The Motion Picture* and nearly a decade and a half before helming the sappy family drama *7th Heaven* for eleven seasons. The show also featured Roddy McDowell as Bon Chance Louie, a sort of take on Claude Rains' Louis from *Casablanca*. Meanwhile, over on CBS's *Bring 'Em Back Alive*, we got Frank Buck, played by Bruce Boxleitner, the year before he became Scarecrow to Kate Jackson's Mrs. King. Frank Buck was a big game hunter who also fought the bad guys from his homebase in 1930's Singapore.

I recall watching both of these shows rather avidly back in my youth. My 13 year old self enjoyed both thoroughly, as would most any 13 year old boy of the time, but preferred *Tales of the Gold Monkey*. I suppose that was the sillier of the two, hence making it more fun for this 13 year old kid in 1982. It was the better reviewed of the two also. *Bring 'Em Back Alive* was actually based on a book by the real life Frank Buck, while *Tales* was based on the 1939 Howard Hawks film, *Only Angels Have Wings*, which in turn inspired the Disney animated TV show, *TaleSpin*. Eventually both series ran out of steam and were cancelled by season's end, airing their last episodes just a night apart.

Not Necessarily the News (1983-90)

Years before *The Daily Show*. Years before *The Colbert Report*. Years before *Last Week Tonight*. Years before *Fox News*. Years before any of these fake news shows came on the air, there was *Not Necessarily the News*. Premiering as an HBO comedy special in September 1982, and then as a regular weekly series on HBO for 8 seasons, from 1983 to 1990, *Not Necessarily the News* was the grandaddy of all those fake news shows that seem to sprout up every month or so.

Inspired by the British series, *Not the Nine O'Clock News*, which ran from 1979 to 1982, the format of the show was pretty much the same as the aforementioned shows which followed it, full of funny news stories and topical political satire. The show featured many of the top up-and-coming sketch comics of the day including one of the first television appearances by later *SNL* regular Jan Hooks. Rich Hall, who had just come off of *Fridays* (also in this book) and would go on to be on *SNL* as well, was one of the main cast members, along with Ann Bloom, Danny Breen, Mitchell Laurence, Stuart Pankin, and Lucy Webb. Hall left the show in 1984 to do *Saturday Night Live*, but returned to *NNTN* after his one and only season on NBC's Saturday night sketch show.

Comic genius and Emmy Award winner Harry Shearer, also of *SNL*, as well as *This is Spinal Tap*, and later as a multitude of voices on *The Simpsons* (Mr. Burns, Ned Flanders, Reverend Lovejoy just to name a few), joined the cast for its final season. The show is also noted for giving the first ever writing credit to future late night legend, Conan O'Brien. The original format lasted until 1989, when the show went to live format for it's last few months. The final episode was a 1990 HBO special entitled, *Not Necessarily the Year in Review*. Today it is mostly forgotten, but if it were not for *Not Necessarily the News*, we would not have had *The Daily Show* and all of it's ilk. And the world would be a lesser place without them. Well, we might have been better off without the made-up nonsense over at *Fox News*, but even that fake news network owes a debt of gratitude to *Not Necessarily the News*. Hell, *Fox News* could use that title as a slogan.

Wizards & Warriors (1983)

When this show first aired, back on February 26, 1983, I was very excited. That excitement kept strong through all eight episodes of this CBS midseason replacement. Then, on May 14 of the same year, as quickly as it first appeared, the show ceased to be. I was probably devastated. Who knows for sure? You see, shortly after this, as far as I can tell, I totally forgot all about this fantasy-comedy show. I probably moved onto some new televised obsession of the day, and left this poor forgotten show behind. I mean, *Manimal* did debut the next season. But I digress.

As quickly as it ceased to be in the prime time television schedule, this show ceased to be in my then fifteen year old mind as well. I would not think about it again for another thirty plus years, while I was digging around the internet for choice fodder for this book. So, when I stumbled across this long forgotten teenage memory, I of course, had to go back and watch all eight episodes, just to see if my faded memories were accurate. And you know what? It was just as silly, and just as exhilarating now, as I remember it being then. Of course, as I already stated, I did not remember much. A show that even I forgot. Howzabout that?

Created, written, and produced by Don Reo, the mind behind the creation of *Blossom* seven years later (one must ask oneself if this is something of which to be proud?), *Wizards & Warriors* was the story of two warring kingdoms and the ongoing battles between the good Prince Erik Greystone and the evil Prince Dirk Blackpool. The good Prince Erik was played by *Taxi* and *Grease* alum, Jeff Conaway. Evil Prince Dirk was played by Canadian actor and figure skater, Duncan Regehr. The show also featured Julia Duffy as spoiled Princess Ariel, who after this show was cancelled would be cast in *Newhart*, for which she would receive seven consecutive Primetime Emmy nominations for Best Supporting Actress – all while playing basically the modern day version of her spoiled princess here.

Even though the show was cancelled due to low ratings, it was, at least a little bit, critically acclaimed. The reviews were mostly positive in the day. It even won an Emmy for Outstanding Costumes for a Series. But today, even by this author, who loved the show as a kid (and as an adult), has been long forgotten – which is sad, because it wasn't half bad. It was just in the wrong place at the wrong time. In today's post *Game of Thrones* world, who knows what fate it would have had?

Manimal (1983)

When the highlight of your show biz career is an eight week stint playing a doctor who can shape shift into an animal and fight crime, then you know you are one of the greats. Wow, that was a bit on the bitchy side. My deepest apologies to British thespian Simon MacCorckindale. After all, he did have a major role in *Jaws 3D*. Still bitchy? Yeah, sorry about that. Seriously though, Mr. MacCorkindale, did follow *Manimal* up with a long run on the hit prime time soap, *Falcon Crest*. Incidentally, he also played a con man, impersonating English cousin Gaylord Duke in an episode of *The Dukes of Hazzard*. Wow, poor Mr. MacCorkindale is really taking a hit today. But seriously, there are worse career highlights than being a shape shifting crimefighter on NBC for eight weeks in 1983. There could be that Gaylord Duke thing. Ouch. I digress.

MacCorkindale, who was seriously a perfectly fine actor (sorry for the ribbing Simon), played Dr. Jonathan Chase, an NYU professor of animal behavioral science, who inherited the ability to shape shift into any animal from his now late father, in some far off jungle somewhere. Dr. Chase also worked with the NYPD, solving crimes and tracking down the bad guys as only he could. All is explained (sort of) at the beginning of each episode by actor William Conrad (*Cannon, Jake and the Fatman*) in voiceover: "Dr Jonathan Chase... wealthy, young, handsome. A man with the brightest of futures. A man with the darkest of pasts. From Africa's deepest recesses, to the rarefied peaks of Tibet, heir to his father's legacy and the world's darkest mysteries. Jonathan Chase, master of the secrets that divide man from animal, animal from man... Manimal!" foreboding, huh?

The show was the brainchild (not sure if that is the proper term for what this show was) of TV veteran Glen A. Larson, the man who also gave the world *Battlestar Galactica, B.J. and the Bear, Quincy M.E., The Fall Guy, Magnum P.I.*, and *Knight Rider*. Larson's second mistake, after the obvious first one of creating the show in the first place, was allowing NBC to schedule his show on Friday nights opposite the number one ratings juggernaut that was *Dallas* on CBS. Granted, this was more the network's mistake than Larson's, as they were the ones with all the power in this television game. But was it a mistake? Come on, think about it. They had to put something opposite *Dallas*, so why not a show you know is going to fail anyway? Why waste a quality show in that kind of death spot? Which brings up another valid question. Why the hell did NBC even pick up *Manimal* in the first place? Was it Larson's successful track record that made the network take a chance on a show about a shape shifting crimefighter? Or was it just that they could not find anything better during pilot season? Wow, if that were the case, just imagine how bad the shows they turned down were. For example, there was *After George*, which starred Susan Saint James as a widow who finds out her late husband programmed his being into the computer system that operates their house. But alas, this modern day take on *My Mother the Car*, was not picked up in order for NBC to allow room on their schedule for *Manimal*. But again, I digress.

The show also starred Melody Anderson, best know for portraying Dale Arden in the 1980 cult classic *Flash Gordon*, as Police Detective Brooke Mackenzie, one of only two people to be aware of Jonathan's unique abilities. The other character in on

Jonathan's animalistic secret identity was Ty Earl, Simon's BFF and crimefighting partner. Ty was played by Michael D. Roberts, best known as the pimp Rooster on the ABC detective show *Baretta*. And since we're playing that game, Robert's career highlight may be his appearance on an episode of *Good Times* as a character named Neck-Bone. But once again, I digress. Let's stop taking cheap hacks at the actors and swing that critical hatchet at the show itself. *Manimal* has the distinction of finding a spot on pretty much every worst of TV list ever made. I challenge you to find a list of the worst shows of all-time without *Manimal* on it. To be completely honest, I don't believe it can be done.

So, I suppose by now, you've gleaned that this author and TV critic & historian, is not the biggest fan of *Manimal*. Don't get me wrong, as a lifelong science fiction fan and comic book aficionado, I love the concept of the show. A take on the DC Comic Animal Man. And yes, there are several other equally awful shows in this book that I am a fan of. Just wait till you get to the chapter on the godawfully wonderful *Cop Rock*. But alas, I could never get behind *Manimal*. It was probably the lack of effort by pretty much everyone involved. Seriously, why when a man has the ability to turn into any damn animal he so desires, save for less than a handful of times, we only ever see him transform into a black panther or a hawk? I realize the budget probably wasn't all that high, but still. There was that one time he turned into a snake in order to save Brooke from one of those most dangerous of TV and film tropes, the dreaded quicksand. I think he may have turned into a dolphin once too. But the panther and hawk were his all too often go to creature features. Maybe the producers knew someone who owned a panther and a hawk. Who knows? And then there was that transformation.

First MacCorkindale would begin heavily breathing, and then the slow and laboured transformation would begin. Ever so slowly he would change, all the while people were in mortal danger from criminals with guns or that dreaded all-encompassing quicksand. These transformations, which went on for seeming ever, seemed to take up half the show – and there were not many of them. And to think, these transformative special effects were created by four time Academy Award winner Stan Winston, the creative f/x mind behind such sci-fi works as *Jurassic Park, Aliens, Predator*, and *Edward Scissorhands*.

Thankfully though, after the awful writing, the awful production, the awful acting (yeah, there goes that hatchet wielding again), and the general awfulness of the show as a whole (I will happily concede the special effects were not all that awful, even if they were portrayed in such an awful narrative manner), after all this, and after eight excruciating episodes, the show was at last put out of it's, and our, misery sooner than later. We do get to meet Dr. Jonathan Chase one more time though. In a 1998 episode of Glen Larson's comic book adaptation *Night Man*, MacCorkindale reprises his role one last time. *Manimal* also ended up spawning an almost nine minute long segment on Late Night with David Letterman, where the show is relentlessly slaughtered by Letterman and his gang of irregulars. At one point, Letterman brings in a psychic to see if NBC will ever bring the show back, getting the response "nope, not on another network, not in syndication, not on home cassettes… it's a ghost, it's history, it's vapor." I need say no more.

W*A*L*T*E*R (1984)

This show has the distinction of having one of the shortest runs of any show in this book. In fact, it ran for exactly one episode. And that episode had exactly one broadcast. Hard to top that, huh? Anyway, this extremely short run show, which in all reality was nothing more than a pilot, desperately hoping to one day become a show, was one of those shoulda coulda woulda type things.

The story, which acts as the second spinoff of the CBS hit series *M*A*S*H*, revolves around the 4077th's one time company clerk, Cpl Walter "Radar" O'Reilly, after he returned home to Iowa. We find out that Radar fails at becoming a farmer, sells the farm and ships his mother off to live with her sister, and ships himself off to St. Louis to become a police officer with his cousin Wendall. All this happens prior to the happenings of the pilot. The pilot revolves around journalist Clete Roberts, a real life war correspondent who played himself in several episodes of *M*A*S*H*, interviewing Walter, who no longer goes by Radar, for a TV special on all the former members of the 4077th. We get to see interviews with Hawkeye on Rad…um I mean on Walter's television set. There are other storylines in the show, including being left at the altar and even thoughts of suicide. A strange take for a comedy of that day, but then *M*A*S*H* hit on many heady topics in its later years, including what war does to a person's psyche. But mostly, the pilot just keeps hitting the viewer over the head with the connection between this show and the aforementioned *M*A*S*H*.

From its pedigree alone, *W*A*L*T*E*R* should have been picked up. I mean really, after eleven smash seasons of *M*A*S*H*, winning ratings and awards galore, one of the most critically acclaimed and well respected television shows of all-time, and with Gary Burghoff's Cpl. Walter 'Radar' O'Reilly being at the center of much of that, one would think that his own spin-off would kind of be a no-brainer. Of course this pilot did not come about until the first season of *AfterMASH*, the actual spin-off of *M*A*S*H*, had completed. Even though that show was renewed for a second season, it was not the big hit CBS was hoping for, and perhaps the network did not want to take the chance on a second spin-off. Then again, perhaps it was never picked up because it was just a godawful bad show. Yeah, I'm going to go with the second thing. Just godawful bad. Boring as all get out. Granted, *AfterMASH* was not *M*A*S*H* either, but it at least had a few laughs. *W*A*L*T*E*R* on the other hand. Well you can watch its one episode on Youtube and make up your own mind on the show's godawfulness. But trust me, you'll end up agreeing with me on this. *W*A*L*T*E*R* is a show better left forgotten.

The Duck Factory (1984)

In 1990, Fox Television gave us the sketch comedy show, *In Living Color*. This hit variety-esque show would give the world the Wayans Brothers, Oscar winner Jamie Foxx, and superstar comic actor, Jim Carrey. But it was six years before *In Living Color*, when Jim Carrey had experienced his first taste of being a leading man, even if it was for just 13 lousy episodes. *The Duck Factory* debuted on NBC in April of 1984, acting as a midseason replacement for the critically acclaimed *Buffalo Bill*, a series that was canceled after just one and a half seasons, only to be nominated for a Best Comedy Series Emmy after it was canceled. At least *Buffalo Bill* had that going for it. The poor hapless *Duck Factory* never even had that during, or after, its thirteen week run on the Peacock Network. It didn't help that it had to go up against *Cheers*, the show that would actually go on to win that Emmy for which the aforementioned *Buffalo Bill* had been nominated. It also probably didn't help much that the show was rather tepid and not all that funny, even with the usually hilarious Mr. Carrey at its chewy nougat center. Which is ironic, since the show was about people who wrote jokes for a living.

The situation comedy was created by Allen Burns, the man who had already given us *The Munsters*, *The Mary Tyler Moore Show*, and *Rhoda*. The setting is the low-budget animation company of Buddy Winkler Productions, the makers of "The Dippy Duck Show." Carrey's naive Skip Tarkenton gets a job as an animator in the company, nicknamed The Duck Factory. The show also featured veteran comic Jack Gilford, and actual cartoon voice legend Don Messick, who you may have heard as Bamm-Bamm Rubble, Scooby-Doo, Boo-Boo Bear, and Papa Smurf, among many others. Even though it had all the tried and true trappings that made for a successful sitcom, the show was just a silly attempt at situational comedy, and was cancelled after it's July 11, 1984 episode. Today, even though Jim Carrey may very well be a household name, *The Duck Factory* is long gone from most people's memories, which may not be such a bad thing after all.

E/R (1984-85)

Who here can recall that one time emergency room set show that starred George Clooney? No, not that one! The other one! That's right, kids. The long-running NBC medical drama, *ER*, was not Mr. George Clooney's first ER show. No sir. A full decade before the more famous *ER* came on the air, there was a sitcom on CBS, called *E/R*. While NBC's drama ran for a whopping 15 seasons, this *E/R* ran for just a single 22 episode season. But yeah, both took place in a hospital ER, both were named *ER* (or technically *E/R* in the comedy's case), and both starred George Clooney. Of course, one of these shows obviously has no business being in a book about forgotten TV shows, so let's concentrate on the one season wonder for this chapter.

Okay, first of all, we should probably get something cleared up. Sure, George Clooney was the star of that second *ER*, but his participation in the first *E/R* may have been a bit exaggerated in my opening salvo. Technically, the star of *E/R* was Elliott Gould. Clooney would not even show up until episode 14, but his name suckered ya'll in, so ya might as well keep reading at this point. The show's actual leading man was Academy Award nominee Gould, already a big name star of stage and screen. Gould starred as Dr,. Howard Sheinfeld, a snide emergency room doctor with a heart of gold, reminiscent of the doctors from *M*A*S*H*, one of whom the actor originated in the 1970 Robert Altman film. Also aboard was the by-the-books head doc Eve Sheridan (played my *Welcome Back Kotter*'s Marcia Strassman in the pilot, but replaced by Mary McDonnell in the series), and nurses Joan Thor (Conchata Ferrell) and Julie Williams (Lynn Moody).

This ER show, of course, revolved around the goings on in a busy city emergency room, more specifically in Chicago's fictional Clark Street Hospital's emergency room. Mainly a comedy, the show did have its dramatic moments, just like the aforementioned *M*A*S*H*. A very well written show, highlighted by Gould's ability to combine his wry sense of humor with a sense of medical drama pathos, it was nonetheless cancelled after just 22 episodes. It didn't help the show that CBS put it on opposite ratings juggernaut *The A-Team* over on NBC.

As I said before, and what may have suckered you in, George Clooney also appeared on this show, albeit as a recurring character in just the final eight episodes. The actor, in his first credited screen appearance, played Ace Kolmar, Nurse Thor's nephew and an ER tech. The show also featured a pre-*Seinfeld* Jason Alexander as a hospital administrator. This show is obviously not as remembered as that other *ER* show starring Mr. Clooney, which incidentally also featured his co-star here, Mary McDonnell, in 5 episodes (and an Emmy nomination for Outstanding Guest Actress), and was also set in a Chicago hospital, but it's lack of being remembered should not sell short it's underappreciated quality. Clooney, would later go on to recurring roles in both *The Facts of Life* and *Roseanne*, before heading into that other *ER* show, and maybe some Hollywood fame, an Oscar, and general all-around movie stardom.

1st & Ten (1984-91)

Long before shows like *The Sopranos* and *Sex and the City*, *Game of Thrones* and *Veep*, *True Detective* and *Boardwalk Empire*, put HBO on the map of hit original series, the network, which originally stood for Home Box Office, was just a place to watch hit Hollywood movies, risque stand-up comedy specials, and big name boxing matches. But in 1984, a dozen years after the cable network's launch, they decided to try their hand at something that up until then, had pretty much been the exclusive domain of network broadcast television - the situation comedy. The show was called *1st & Ten*, and it was a raunchy, often bacchanalian satire on pro football. Sure, HBO had begun airing original programming the previous year, in the form of the (kinda) kids show *Fraggle Rock*, the horror anthology *The Hitchhiker*, the docuseries *America Undercover*, and the political sketch comedy show, *Not Necessarily the News* (also included in this book), but *1st & Ten* was not only the cable network's first attempt at a sitcom, but also something different, something a bit more groundbreaking - at least for the time period.

Delta Burke starred as Diane Barrow, who after catching her football team owning husband in flagrante delicto with one of his tight ends, gets awarded said team, The California Bulls, in the ensuing divorce. And hence, this was the crux of the show. Doing what you couldn't do on one of the "Big Three" networks, *1st & Ten* swore, got nasty, and showed a bit of nudity. But the show was more than just that. Those bits were just added benefits, proving HBO could do things the other networks could not. Despite the raunchiness (which incidentally was still rather tame when compared to more modern HBO programming) the show was actually rather smartly written, showing the difficulties of being a woman in what was a very male-dominated business like professional football. It was a feminist take on misogyny – well, except for maybe when the topless bouncing cheerleaders would come running through the scene as if Yakety Sax was playing.

Also taking on subjects such as drug use in football and the interference of organized crime and gambling in the sport, *1st & Ten* was a powerhouse of satirical comedy at the time. Season two saw the addition of O.J. Simpson to the cast. Nine years prior to that "incident" at Simpson's condo in Brentwood, O.J. was known merely as one of the biggest names in NFL history, and his inclusion was nothing short of a ratings boost through the proverbial roof. To be fair, I'm sure including O.J. in a TV show now would make the ratings go through the roof as well, but probably in a more morbid curiosity way, and a less hero worship kinda way.

Delta Burke would leave the show midway through season three to concentrate on her new show on CBS, *Designing Women*. This didn't stop the original premise of a woman owning a pro football team though. Through circumstances throughout the rest of it's six season run, the Bulls would almost always be owned by a woman. Unfortunately though, after Burke's departure, the show devolved into basically *Police Academy* on the football field. The integral combination of the show's smart and witty writing and raunchy sexy humour of the first two seasons, gave way to just raunchier humour and less and less wit as each of the final four seasons progressed. For it's groundbreaking beginnings, *1st & Ten* should be better remembered than it is today, which is basically not at all.

Moonlighting (1985-89)

This ABC dramedy is one of my favourite shows in this whole book. And the critics of the day might just agree with me. And maybe the viewers too. Yes, *Moonlighting* is mostly forgotten today (why else would I be talking about in this book), but it was both a critical and popular darling when it was on. After starting out as a midseason replacement during the 1984-85 season, *Moonlighting* hit its stride in season two, where it tied for 20th place in the Nielsen ratings and was nominated for 16 Emmy Awards. Season three brought a peak at 9th place in the ratings and another 14 Emmy nominations. Season four saw a 12th place finish and another 13 Emmy nominations. The show's fifth and final season saw everything decline, but more on that in a bit. Let's talk about the show itself.

Moonlighting was something not seen on TV that often at the time. It was a comedy, a situation comedy, but also had dramatic moments, and action sequences too. *Moonlighting* was what one would call film noir, or at least neo-noir. But it was also a hoot. Taking it's cue from classic Hollywood films like *The Big Sleep* and *The Maltese Falcon*, *Moonlighting* was a hard-nosed detective show, but a funny hard-nosed detective show, with the fast-paced dialogue of an old Screwball Comedy of the 1930's. And it was also a romance of sorts as well. Created by Glenn

Gordon Caron, one of the main writers on the similarly themed Remington Steele, the show was a unique blend of all these genres – and it worked.

The show was also a meta something or other, breaking the fourth wall on the regular. Sometimes addressing the audience directly, other times by discussing the producers or writers or even the network itself, all the while knowingly winking at the audience (much in the way Ryan Reynolds would later do in the *Deadpool* films) always self-aware that they were merely characters in a TV show. Pierce Brosnan even jumped networks to make a cameo as his Remington Steele character. In a nod to the finale Mel Brooks' *Blazing Saddles*, sometimes the action would leave the set altogether, and move out and into other parts of the studio, even interfering in other TV shows being shot. And that was just part of the fantastical aspect of the show. *Moonlighting* was full of dream sequences and dance numbers and even a Shakespeare adaptation once. There was one episode even done in the black and white of old film noir. The network made them put a disclaimer at the beginning of this episode as to not have modern day audiences confused by the lack of colour. This episode was even filmed on black and white stock, to stop the network from forcing them to air the colour version instead. Orson Welles narrated this black and white episode, which aired just two days after the legendary director passed away.

I guess we should talk about the stars of this strange and delightful program while we're here. The show starred Cybill Shepherd, already a name in modelling and in movies, as Maddie Hayes, a chic former model who is left bankrupt after her accountant embezzles her fortune, and is forced to run the detective agency she once bought as a tax write-off. Shepherd leapt at the role after reading the script, calling it Hawksian in nature. Some of the actresses favourite films were the screwball comedies of Howard Hawks, like *His Girl Friday* and *Bringing Up Baby* – which Shepherd made everyone watch to prepare for the first season. Her romantic foil on the show was David Addison, a wisecracking detective working at said detective agency. Addison was played by an unknown 29 year old actor by the name of Bruce Willis. Yeah, that Bruce Willis. Willis beat out more than 2000 other actors to win the part. At first, ABC didn't want to take the chance on the actor, as they didn't think he and Shepherd would have any chemistry together. Boy were they wrong. The duo's smoking chemistry was one of the best things about the show. Allyce Beasley and Curtis Armstrong, as Agnes DiPesto and Herbert Viola respectively, were also in the cast, and these four made up Blue Moon Investigations.

The show was also full of guest stars galore, like the aforementioned Mr. Orson Welles and Pierce Brosnan, and including, but not limited to, Mark Harmon, Virginia Madsen, Eva Marie Saint, Tim Robbins, C. Thomas Howell, Billy Barty, Mary Hart, Dana Delaney, Richard Belzer, Judd Nelson, Whoopi Goldberg, Paul Sorvino, Cheryl Tiegs, John Goodman, Ray Charles, Imogene Coca, Demi Moore (who was Willis' new wife at the time), Timothy Leary, and even The Temptations. While it was on, *Moonlighting* was the cool place to be, and all the stars knew that. A popular and critically acclaimed show that was so innovative and so groundbreaking in its production. But alas, nothing lasts forever.

Yes, *Moonlighting* was definitely a success for it's first four seasons. Consistently good ratings and an overall count of 40

Emmy nominations and 7 Emmy victories, including one for Bruce Willis for Outstanding Actor in a Drama Series. But then came that fifth season. When Shepherd and Willis returned for the fifth season, neither's heart was into it anymore. Shepherd had newborn twins at home and was overwhelmed by the workload of a weekly hour long series. Meanwhile Willis was flying high on the success of *Die Hard*, and was looking forward to a movie career. Neither actor wanted to be there and it showed on the screen. The chemistry was gone. The wit was drying up. It was the beginning of the end. By May of 1989, the show was off the air. In keeping with the irreverent spirit of the show, the final episode has Maddie & David returning to find the Blue Moon set being torn apart and an ABC executive telling them they were cancelled. The show was never really shown all that much in syndication, and therefore has been left to the wayside, and forgotten. But I still say this may be the best damn show in this book, and deserves a better fate than being included in this book in the first place, other than just as a trivia question on where Bruce Willis got his start.

Misfits of Science (1985-86)

Before she became a household name in *Friends* in 1994, and not that long after she was pulled up on stage by The Boss in Springsteen's Dancing in the Dark video, a 21 year old Courtney Cox was featured in that spectacular hit series, *Misfits of Science*. Um…ok, so it was far from spectacular and far from a hit, but the part about Courtney Cox being in it is true. Save for a single episode of the daytime drama, *As the World Turns*, *Misfits of Science* was the actresses first television role. Cox would go on to star as Alex P. Keaton's girlfriend in the final two seasons of the hit series, *Family Ties*, and then, of course, as Monica Geller-Bing on the smash series *Friends*. I am guessing the producers of those shows did not hire Cox from seeing her in *Misfits of*

Science. In fact, they probably never actually saw the show in the first place.

The show, which ran on NBC for 16 episodes between October 1985 and May 1986 (which was probably about 17 too many), was about a group of super-powered humans and their so-called amazing madcap adventures saving the world and all that. Trying to recreate what Stephen J. Cannell did with *The Greatest American Hero* from 1981 to 1983, creator James D. Parriott put together this rag tag team on this rag tag show. He had a shrinking man (Kevin Peter Hall, who's great height would later allow him to play The Predator in that franchise, and Harry in *Harry and the Hendersons*), an electrically powered rock star (Mark Thomas Miller), and a telekinetic teen (the aforementioned Ms. Cox). They were led by a non-powered scientist played by Dean Paul Martin, the son of Rat Packer Dean Martin. Already experienced in the superhero genre (he had been a writer on The *Six Million Dollar Man*, *The Bionic Woman*, *Gemini Man*, and *The Incredible Hulk*) Parriott decided to swing for the fences with this show. Instead he struck out on three pitches.

One might gather, from several disparaging pot shots I've already taken at the show, that I am not a fan of *Misfits of Science*. If one gathered that, one may be correct. Very correct. There are some shows in this book that deserve a second chance, having been forgotten due, not to lack of quality, but a lack of luck or marketing or what have you. I can guarantee the reader that *Misfits of Science* ix not one of these shows. Other than watching out of curiosity of seeing a baby Courtney Cox, or in order to mock it in a *Mystery Science Theater 3000* kinda way, there is no good reason to ever watch this show. *Misfits of Science* deserves to be forgotten – not that I am letting you do that. But it is a fun lark (for quick short bursts) for fans of *Friends*.

Max Headroom (1987-88)

Most of my generation, the generation which came of age in the early to mid 1980's, surely remembers the pop icon known as Max Headroom. From introducing videos on MTV, back when the music channel actually played music videos (yeah, that was a thing back in the day), to shilling for New Coke, the seemingly computer generated Max Headroom was all over your TV. Well, at least all over the TV's of those hip enough to be watching channels like MTV, back when the music channel was actually a hip thing to watch. But does anyone actually remember the TV show that was spawned from this pop cultural icon? Nope? Didn't think so. Well, let's talk a little bit about that show, shall we?

Max Headroom, the character, made his first appearance on April 4, 1985, on the British-made cyberpunk TV movie *Max Headroom: 20 Minutes into the Future*. Max would next appear on the UK music video program, *The Max Headroom Show*, a sort of British take on MTV, which aired from 1985 until Spring of 1987. Then, on March 31, 1987, just a few weeks after the British series went off the air, the US series first appeared on ABC. Moving away from the music video aspect of the character's past (though he could still be found on MTV in his veejay persona) this new series was a sci-fi series set in a dystopian future ruled by an oligarchy of fascist television networks. The premise for the show was based on the original UK TV movie.

The story went a little something like this. In the future, the world is controlled by the CEO's of a few television networks, who also control the puppet governments they have placed in so-called power, have outlawed any non-television technology, and spy on people through their TV's, which by the way, they are not allowed or even able to turn off. The only real check on the power of the networks is crusading TV journalist, Edison Carter. Meanwhile, after recuperating from a motorcycle accident, Carter's mind is reconstructed via a computer program and placed into a computer rendered bust of the journalist who calls himself Max Headroom. The last sight Carter recalls before the accident was a sign warning him of the maximum head room of a parking garage. So, while a recovered Carter keeps up his crusade against the man, Max acts as a spokesman for the man, but still maintaining some semblance of Carter's ideals inside of his circuits.

Both Carter and Max were portrayed by the relatively unknown Matt Frewer. Frewer would later appear in many films and TV shows, most notably in the 2004 Zack Snyder *Dawn of the Dead* remake, the Stephen King TV adaptation *The Stand*, and most recently as a regular on the AMC series *Fear the Walking Dead*. Amanda Pays, another relative unknown, and the future scientist and love interest of Barry Allen in the 1990 TV incarnation of *The Flash* (a role she would reprise in the updated CW series of the same name), played Theora Jones, Carter's boss and wrangler, and would be love interest. This would be love story never gets to amount to much (Pays character's love never pays off) as the show would be cancelled before this subplot storyline was ever able to get off the ground.

Speaking of cancellation. The show began as a midseason replacement in early 1987 and was eventually renewed for a second season, only to be placed on hiatus midway through that second season and eventually cancelled after it temporarily returned to the prime time line-up in the Spring of 1988. The show itself, TV's original cyberpunk tale, was solid storytelling, with the comic relief of Max Headroom being the highlight, but one supposes it's cancellation was inevitable when it had to go up against ratings champs *Dallas* on CBS and *Miami Vice* on NBC. In the end, this show may not be all that memorable, but Max Headroom, who worked better as ad pitch man and part time MTV veejay, lives on in the hearts and minds of Generation X – which may explain a lot about the mental stability of my generation.

Remote Control (1987-90)

From one MTV inspired show, to another. In December of 1987, just a little over six years after MTV was first launched upon the television watching public, the upstart network with the cool attitude, decided to produce their first non-music-related program. Yes, today one would be hard-pressed to find a music video on the once-heralded music channel (officially, the M no longer stands for music, it's just an M), but thirty years ago, back in the network's early heyday, it was nothing but music, twenty-four seven. So with a bit of derring-do, the powers that be at Viacom, the media conglomerate that had bought the network two years earlier, *Remote Control* was launched. Other non-music programs, such as *House of Style*, and *The Real World* would begin popping up over the next few years, but it was *Remote Control* that ushered in this new era. Gee thanks.

Being a part of MTV, and therefore aiming toward a mostly younger generation (the contestants were all college students), the show was meant to be an irreverent style game show, revolving around music, movies, TV, and general pop culture. Generation X's answer to the supposedly stuffier game shows of the Baby Boomer generation. This meant the show had no real structure, with fluctuating rules and a loose sense of scoring, and an in your face 1980's attitude, which worked perfectly well for what the show, and what the network, was trying to be at the time. And it also made the show a fun romp had by all.

Ken Ober, who had been a stand-up comic contestant on Star Search in 1984, was the host of the show. The premise was that "Little Kenny" was desperate to have his own game show, so he set one up in his mother's basement. As the theme song went, "Kenny wasn't like the other kids / TV mattered, nothing else did / Girls said yes, but he said no / Now he's got his own game show." With a basement set full of typical basement décor, pop culture kitsch, including a giant Bob Eubanks Pez dispenser, a washer & dryer, three giddy contestants, a snarky sidekick, a revolving door of pretty girls, and music & mayhem galore, Ober would put on his irreverent game show for all to see and enjoy.

Ober was joined in his mother's basement each week by future *SNL* Weekend Update anchor Colin Quinn as the aforementioned snarky sidekick. Quinn was also a writer on the show, as were both stand-up comic Denis Leary and Adam Sandler, the latter of whom left the show to join the cast of *Saturday Night Live*, both of whom played various characters throughout the show's time on the air. There was also that bevy of pretty girls. This revolving door of show hostesses were Marisol Massey (season 1), Kari Wührer (seasons 2 & 3), Alicia Coppola (season 4), and Susan Ashley (season 5). Full of fun and frivolity, the show revolved around pop culture questions given to three contestants. Sometimes these were straight forward questions, sometimes they were skits and comedy routines. At one point, the third place contestant was tossed from the room via the leather recliners they were seat-belted into, and the final two battled it out in a lightning round, before the winner would go on to try their hand at the bonus round. The whole thing was a blast.

Nipsey Russell, the so-called Port Laureate of Television, was a semi-regular on the show, who would come on to recite his poetry as portions of questions. Other celebrities who appeared on the show, sometimes as guests, sometimes as contestants (sometime as one and then in a later episode as the other), included the likes of MC Hammer, LL Cool J, Barry Williams, Eve Plumb, & Susan Olsen from *The Brady Bunch*, Jerry "The Beaver" Mathers, and "Weird Al" Yankovic. After 5 seasons on the air (but in only 3 years, due to seasons and time acting differently on MTV), the show aired it's final episode on December 13, 1990. Ober would go onto other hosting gigs, and became a producer on TV, most notably as one of the producers on the CBS comedy, *The New Adventures of Old Christine*. Sadly, Ober passed away on November 15, 2009, at the age of 52. Both Ober and his show should be remembered.

Hooperman (1987-89)

Although there were comedy-drama hybrids before it, this ABC dramedy, which debuted on September 23, 1987, and would last for two seasons on the alphabet network, was considered by many to be the first of it's kind, so much so, that the term "dramedy" was actually coined to describe the show. Others of this so-called new genre began showing up in the years to come. Shows like *Northern Exposure, Ally McBeal, Gilmore Girls, Weeds, Shameless,* and *Orange is the New Black.* Even though the term was coined by critics describing *Hooperman*, I can't really attest to this being the real starting point of the dramedy, as shows such as *Moonlighting* existed before it. One could even go back to 1969 and *Room 222*. One could also include such hit situation comedies as *All in the Family* and *M*A*S*H*, as dramedies of their day. Even a show such as *The Nights & Days of Molly Dodd*, a show that could easily be included in this book (maybe volume 2), and which debuted just a few months prior to *Hooperman*, could easily count as a dramedy. But I digress. This is not about the merits of a critical TV term, this is about the dramedy in question, *Hooperman*.

After 8 seasons on the hit ABC series *Three's Company*, and finally winning his oh so long overdue Emmy in the show's final season, and another year on the failed spin-off, *Three's a Crowd*, John Ritter found himself the star of his third show. This time around, he was playing a San Francisco police detective named Harry Hooperman. The show split itself up, between Harry's life as a police detective, and all his wacky fellow cops, and with his home life, where he owns an apartment building he inherits from his murdered former landlady in the first episode. The show also included Barbara Bosson, who had just come off 7 seasons of the critically acclaimed *Hill Street Blues*, as the recently divorced Capt. Celeste "C.Z." Stern. The show also featured one of the first openly gay characters on prime time television. Joseph Gian, who a year earlier was named Best Male Vocalist on *Star Search* (the show that gave the world 1980's teen pop sensation Tiffany) played openly gay police officer Rick Silardi. Dan Lauria also appeared as Capt. Stern's ex-hubby, just before he was cast as the patriarch in *The Wonder Years*.

The show also had a slew of guest stars, which included Don Cheadle, a pre-*Frasier* Jane Leeves, and *Growing Pains*' Joanna Kerns, but most notably Norman Fell, who of course, was Mr. Roper on *Three's Company*. The show was created by Steven Bochco & Terry Louise Fisher, the team behind *L.A. Law*, which was one of the hottest shows on TV when *Hooperman* premiered. Incidentally, Bochco was married to Ms. Bosson, who starred in most of her husband's shows. With *Hooperman*'s 35th place ranking in the Nielsen ratings that season (out of 105 shows), ABC renewed the show for a second season, but after it's 57th place finish the following year, a season three would never come. After *Hooperman*, Ritter would go on to star opposite Markie Post in the sitcom *Hearts Afire*, which ran for 3 seasons, from 1992 to 1995, and then in *8 Simples Rules for Dating My Teenage Daughter* in 2002. Sadly, Ritter died suddenly while filming the fourth episode of season two of *8 Simple Rules*. The show went on after the actor's death, but it never again reached the heights it's first season reached. Perhaps *Hooperman* (and probably the aforementioned *Hearts Afire*) has been mostly forgotten, but television legend John Ritter never will be.

Nearly Departed (1989)

As soon as you see *Monty Python* alumni Eric Idle singing and dancing the theme song, you are hooked. Okay, maybe that was just me, because no one else seemed to be hooked. Lasting a lousy 4 episodes in the Spring of 1989 (plus another 2 unaired) appearing and disappearing like the apparition it was, this NBC situation comedy updating of the *Topper* films and television series, was about as far from a hit as one could possibly imagine. Even with Eric Idle singing and dancing through the intro, no one ever got hooked – except for maybe me.

As I said, this show was an updating of *Topper*, but also an attempt at cashing in on the popularity of the 1988 film *Beetlejuice*. Idle and Caroline McWilliams of *Benson* fame, starred as the late Professor Grant and equally as late Claire Pritchard, who were both killed in a rockslide, only to find themselves as ghosts in their old home, now owned by plumbing contractor named Mike Dooley (Stuart Pankin) and his loving wife Liz (Wendy Schaal), son Derek (Jay Lambert), and his father Jack (Henderson Forsythe). Grandpa Jack is the only living being who can see and hear our not so intrepid ghosts. The show, what there was of it, revolved around the snobby Professor reluctantly helping his still living hosts.

Okay, maybe the show wasn't as great as I was saying in the opening salvo (to be honest, I was only hooked by the intro – once the show started it was all over), but Eric Idle was a highlight of the four aired episodes, and he alone could have kept it all going if given the opportunity. But alas, it was never meant to be, and now the show has long faded away, becoming the ghost it was inevitably meant to be. But seriously, Idle does really suck you in with that theme song intro. You'll be hooked.

Living Dolls (1989-90)

In an earlier chapter, we looked at a sitcom called *My Living Doll*, about a beautiful android making her way through human society. Then, nearly 25 years later ABC television gave us the similarly titled *Living Dolls*, but that is where the similarities end. This much newer situation comedy was actually a spin-off, but not in the traditional sense. It's what we in the biz call a backdoor spin-off or a backdoor pilot. We already discussed this earlier in this book, but just in case you weren't paying attention, here's a quick recap. As opposed to traditional spin-offs such as *The Jeffersons* or *Frasier*, where a regular character, or set of characters, is spun off into their own series, the backdoor version usually introduces characters for just a single episode in the hopes of creating a spin-off. So, in the same way that *Empty Nest* snuck out of *The Golden Girls* and *NCIS* was born from a single episode of *JAG*, *Living Dolls* was created through the 1989 season 5, episode 19 of *Who's the Boss*, titled (appropriately enough) "Living Dolls." From this episode, was spawned the 1989 series.

The story revolves around 16 year old Charlene "Charlie" Briscoe, a former classmate of Alyssa Milano's *Who's the Boss* character Samantha Micelli, who is now a teen model in a Manhattan modeling agency run by Trish Carlin, an old friend of Judith Light's *Boss* character Angela Bower. Trish, who acts as a mother figure to her stable of teen models, was played by five time Emmy Award Winner, Miss Michael Learned of *The Waltons* fame. The teenage models themselves were all unknown at the time, but even though the show was a failure, and is now forgotten, a couple of these unknowns would make it big in Hollywood.

Charlie was played by then 19 year old Leah Remini, who's only screen credit at the time was an episode of ABC's *Head of the Class* and two backdoor episodes of *Who's the Boss*. Remini, of course, would go on to star opposite Kevin James in the hit CBS series *The King of Queens* for 9 hit seasons. The show also featured future Oscar winner Halle Berry in her first ever screen role as Emily. Vivica A. Fox played the part of Emily in the *Who's the Boss* episode, but was replaced by the time the show got on the air. The cast never gels though. Learned, who is well above the material, seems like she is just going through the motions for a paycheck, which was probably exactly the case. Meanwhile, the rest of the show ends up just being a tired *The Facts of Life* retread, with the conceited one, the streetwise one, the innocent one, and the token black girl. The main difference being this show was much worse than *The Facts of Life*, and that is saying a lot. As bad as this show was though, and let's face it, the show was just awful, one could still see the comedic light in the brash Remini. But yeah, the show itself was just godawful.

In comparison with its parent show, *Who's the Boss* was on the air for 8 seasons, from 1984 to 1992, won both Emmys and Golden Globes, was regularly a ratings success, and can still be seen in syndication, and on streaming, to this day. Meanwhile, *Living Dolls*, premiering in September of 1989, barely lasted 12 episodes before being cancelled by Christmas break, and has been almost totally forgotten by everyone, even those few people who actually watched it during it's ever so short run on Saturday nights. In fact, this show is perhaps even more forgotten than many of the shows in this book. I guess I chose the right show to include in this book after all.

Cop Rock (1990)

A cop show that's also a musical? How could this have not been the hit series of the 1990-91 TV season!? Seriously! Yes, the show was panned, and panned big time (think demolished) by critics of the day, and it's often found on those worst shows of all-time lists, but this author, who happens to be a big musical fan, thought it was a grand idea at the time. But it was just too ahead of it's time to work. Yes, I would have loved a cop show that was also a musical, and still would (*Law & Order* missed their chance when they had both song & dance man Jerry Orbach and Jesse Martin from *Rent* on as partners) but the TV watching public just wasn't ready for such a thing in 1990. Perhaps in this day and age, with shows like *Glee* and *My Crazy Ex-Girlfriend* under their belts, and musical theatre being more mainstream, but back then, I suppose not.

It must be noted that *Cop Rock* was the creation of Steven Bochco, the man that gave us the groundbreaking *Hill Street Blues*, the cop show that changed the very face of modern television, and the smash hit series *L.A. Law*, which was at the height of it's popularity, and had already won two of it's eventual four Emmys for Outstanding Drama Series, when *Cop Rock* premiered. How could this go wrong? Well, Bochco was far from perfect, even before the tragedy that was *Cop Rock*. The guy was fired by MTM in 1985 after the complete and utter failure of his baseball comedy series, *Bay City Blues*, which ran for a whole four episodes before being cancelled. But his failure with *Cop Rock* was more legendary than anything else Bochco had failed at.

As I have already stated (and do not take back!) I rather enjoyed the show. Yes, it could have been done better, but Overall it was a fun concept, and an even funner show. Yeah, I said funner! But alas, I suppose audiences were not as enthralled as I had been when, in the middle of a rather intense courtroom scene, the jury got up and did a gospel style rendition of "He's Guilty." Bochco tried to pump up the ratings by bringing some of his more successful crew into the fold. James B. Sikking, who was currently starring in *Doogie Howser, M.D.*, another Bochco creation, reprised his *Hill Street Blues* role of Lt. Howard Hunter in one episode. *L.A. Law* stars Jimmy Smits and Michelle Greene appeared in another. But all this was to no avail, as ABC gave the show the axe after just eleven episodes. Bochco would soon create *NYPD Blue* and be back on top again, but *Cop Rock* would fall into obscurity, save for it's regular appearances on those worst of all-time lists. To me though, it will always be fondly remembered.

Heil Honey, I'm Home (1990)

This British situation comedy may be, not only the most infamous sitcom ever aired, but very likely the most infamous thing ever to appear on television. In fact, this show was so reviled, it was cancelled the morning after it first aired. Eleven episodes were made of the comedy, but only one actually got to see the light of broadcast day. Television historian Marian Calabro described the show as "perhaps the world's most tasteless situation comedy." But just what made this sitcom so hated by everyone who saw it on that singular broadcast on the night of September 30, 1990? Well, here's the premise.

The setting is 1938 Berlin, and the story is the story of suburbanite couple Adolph Hitler and Eva Braun, who live next door to Arny and Rosa Goldenstein, a young Jewish couple. The first episode revolves around Hitler trying to keep his Jewish neighbors away from his house and visiting British Prime Minister, Neville Chamberlain. Yes, that is what the show was. A suburban family sitcom about Hitler and his Jewish neighbors. The show was set up to look like a typical, old time family sitcom, like *I Love Lucy*, strangely it's biggest influence, replete with silly sitcom tropes and a full fledged, and purposely (one assumes, but is not sure) obnoxious laugh track. Did I mention Hitler and Eva Braun speak with Brooklyn accents? Did I mention this was a show about Hitler? Yeah. All this added up to arguably the most hated show in television history. It also added up to no second episode ever reaching the airwaves.

And let's face it, should a second episode have ever aired? Probably not. Creator Geoff Atkinson has tried to claim that he meant no harm, but instead was merely trying to satirize the British appeasement of Hitler before the start of World War II. Atkinson adds that three quarters of the cast were Jewish, and he did not consider the concept controversial. Really? He didn't think a sitcom about Hitler and his Jewish neighbors would be controversial? True, Atkinson, much like Mel Brooks with *The Producers*, probably was trying to mock Hitler himself, but to honestly believe the show was not going to be controversial is probably a bit on the naive side. In the end though, aside from a few WTF articles or video time capsules, this decidedly controversial Britcom has been mostly forgotten. I guess that makes its inclusion here quite appropriate.

<u>Ferris Bueller</u> (1990-91)
<u>Parker Lewis Can't Lose</u> (1990-93)

On August 23, 1990, a new TV show premiered on NBC. It was called *Ferris Bueller*, and it was the television adaptation of the hit 1986 movie, *Ferris Bueller's Day Off*, directed by John Hughes and starring Matthew Broderick. Ten days later, over on the still budding Fox Network, another new show made its debut. This one was called *Parker Lewis Can't Lose*, and it was more than a blatant rip-off of the aforementioned hit 1986 movie. So blatant, that I am surprised there weren't lawsuits flying around in the late Summer of 1990. Especially when one considers how *Ferris Bueller*, the more "official" seeming (no, John Hughes had nothing to do with the show) spinoff of the hit movie lasted a mere 13 episodes and the blatant rip-off ran for three seasons and a total of 73 episodes. To be fair, *Parker Lewis* was the better show, but the *Ferris* TV show didn't exactly put that bar very high.

Since Hughes wasn't involved in the television adaptation of his film, the *Ferris Bueller* TV show was not technically a continuation of the film and it's characters, but rather a portrayal of the real life situations upon which the film was loosely based – or some sort of crap like that. To shove this idea even further down the viewer's gullets, Charlie Schlatter as the titular teen rebel, refers to the film in the pilot episode, and even shows his displeasure of how Mr. Broderick portrayed him in the movie by destroying a life-sized cardboard standee of the actor with a chainsaw. This meta-themed idea was dropped quickly though, as the film was never again mentioned. Schlatter was supposed to be the it kid when he was cast, having just come off the rather tepid but still mild hit film, *18 Again*. This "it" status never really caught on though, and instead Schlatter spent the rest of his career being thought of as the poor man's Christian Slater, with most of his career relegated to voice over work.

Meanwhile, over at the upstart Fox Network, at the same time *Ferris Bueller* was losing and getting itself cancelled, that blatant rip-off, *Parker Lewis Can't Lose*, starring Corin Nemic as Lewis, and much more irreverent and fourth wall breaking than it's competitor, was busy not losing at all. Granted, the Fox show's ratings were never anything to write home about (it did go up against ratings juggernaut *60 Minutes* over on CBS), but since the young network, in only its fourth season in business, was still only programming three nights a week at the time, as opposed to the big three doing seven nights as usual, ratings were not as big a deal to Fox as it was to the others. It didn't hurt that an early internet campaign (so early that the world wide web that we know and love & hate today, was not really a thing yet, and word was still being spread by that newfangled thing called e-mail) by a group calling themselves The Flamingo Digest, after the mascot of the high school portrayed on the show, talked Fox into keeping the show going for a third season.

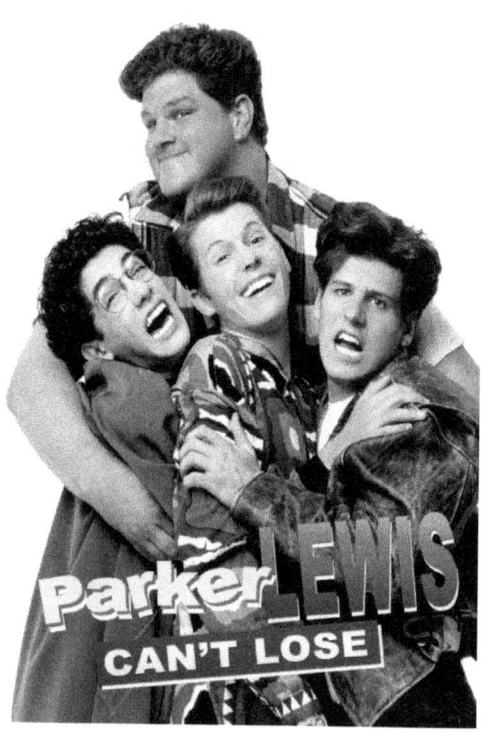

In an interesting aside involving the coincidences of television, the part of Ferris' sister, which had been played by Jennifer Grey on film, was handed to an unknown actress by the name of Jennifer Aniston on the show. A few years later, once Aniston had established herself as a TV force to be reckoned with as Rachel Green on the iconic NBC series *Friends*, the two actresses actually worked together. Aniston as the aforementioned Rachel and Grey as her character's former best friend, and the future wife of the man Rachel had left at the altar in the first episode. The six degrees of separation are indeed a real thing. What is not a real thing is the staying power of either of these shows – even the one that somehow managed to last three seasons. Although the original 1986 film is still a favourite, for not only the Gen Xers who originally saw it as teens (or barely out of their teens), but for the Millennials who came after, no one of any generation remembers either of these copycat shows.

Liquid Television (1991-95)

Ten years before Cartoon Network launched it's Adult Swim programming block, MTV was the place to be for adult-oriented, avant-garde animation. Lasting for 27 sporadic episodes over a three season period, MTV's *Liquid Television* gave the world some of the strangest and some of the most intriguing animated shows ever seen on the small screen. The show, which was originally shown on BBC Two while also showing on MTV, gave a visual voice to many an animator of the day – and put them in a playing field that got their product to a much wider audience than they would have otherwise reached.

The show featured all kinds of animation, from Stick Figure Theatre, where we get stick figure reenactments of hit movies, done on index cards, to Was (Not Was), a series of chalk animation done to the music of the titular one hit wonder band. There was Claymation and computer animation, and even a few segments that were not animated at all, most famously (but not that famously) the puppet theatre of Winter Steele. The show also featured *Æon Flux*, an avant-garde sci-fi series created by Peter Chung, which would spawn off onto it's own series, as well as a series of comic books and a live action motion picture starring Charlize Theron as the kick ass heroine of the story. *Liquid Television*, along with it's successor, *Cartoon Sushi*, which ran for a season in 1997 and 1998, was also the original airer of *The Maxx*, based on the Sam Keith created comic book character, and the Claymation series, *Celebrity Deathmatch*, created by Eric Fogel.

The most famous animation to come from this series though, has got to be the Mike Judge created *Beavis & Butthead*, which spawned an eight season long hit series on MTV, a successful movie, and even it's own spinoff in *Daria* – and was a huge pop culture phenomenon to boot. *Liquid Television* was also the first place anyone ever saw that other Mike Judge animation, *Milton*, which would metamorphose into the live action cult comedy film, *Office Space*. In the end, MTV pulled the plug on *Liquid Television* (and it's aforementioned successor *Cartoon Sushi*), but did launch a website in 2011, wherein you can rewatch many of the show's classic bits, as well as brand new segments. A two episode revival appeared (and quickly disappeared) in the Spring of 2014. This show, thanks to the product that spewed forth from it, is probably a little bit more remembered than most shows in this book. Luckily, remembered or not, unlike many a lost or semi-lost show herein, all of *Liquid Television* can today be viewed online at your leisure.

Herman's Head (1991-94)

Herman's Head, which ran on the Fox Network for 3 seasons, from 1991 to 1994, may have been forgotten by more people than the amount who even watched it in the first place, but the quirky little sitcom does hold a certain unique place in television history. It was during the November 17, 1991 broadcast of the episode "Near-Death Wish," that the first ever condom commercial aired on US television. Of course, this being the best remembered thing about *Herman's Head*, probably doesn't bode well for the quality of the show itself, even if, with 3 seasons and 72 episodes under its belt, it is one of the longer lasting shows in this book.

The premise was simple, and quite intriguing actually. It may be the only situation comedy that can take Freud's concept of the id, the ego, & the super-ego, as one of its major influences. Okay, perhaps that is stretching things a bit, but hyperbole aside, the show was about the conceptual structure of the human psyche, and in a more literal way than had ever been seen on television before. The series was about Herman Brooks, a twentysomething up-and-coming New Yorker (an Ohio-born New York transplant, to be a bit more specific), who worked as a fact checker at a big wig Manhattan magazine publishing firm. Herman is played by William Ragsdale, who was probably best known at the time for playing teen vampire hunter Charley Brewster in the *Fright Night* films. Herman is your typical 1990's sitcom guy. Driven to get ahead, and move from the fact checking first floor to being an actual writer, and driven to get the girl. Any girl, really. Any girl. And to accomplish these things, Herman will do just about anything one would expect a situation comedy guy to do. Yes, there are aspects of *Three's Company*-esque shenanigans to be had here, complete with best bud Jay, via Hank Azaria playing Larry to Herman's oft-times hapless Jack, but the show is not just that. It's actually a lot smarter than that. It's actually a lot smarter than it is often given credit for being.

To get back to that whole aforementioned intriguing premise thing, the basic gist of the show is that we can not only read Herman's thoughts, and feel his emotions, but we can actually meet them as well. And by meet them, I mean that Herman's emotions, his love and anger and fear and even his most basic of animal urges, are played by four actors, supposedly inside of Herman's titular head. Actually, Herman's head looks to be an attic filled with all of Herman's memories, from his childhood family Christmas tree to his college Ohio State pennants to all other kinds of memorabilia from his past. It is in this attic setting where we get to meet Angel (Molly Hagan) who acts as Herman's feminine, sensitive side; Genius (Peter Mackenzie), the intellectual part of his psyche; Wimp (Rick Lawless), Herman's anxiety riddled fear monitor; and Animal (Ken Hudson Campbell), the drunken, lusty, frat boy side of things. These four sides of Herman's head are drawn as one-dimensional archetypes, and find themselves at odds with each other over what Herman should and should not do. There was also a one-time visit from Bobcat Goldthwaite as Herman's Jealousy, and even Leslie Nielsen, in a meta performance as a Leslie Nielsen-looking version of God. And all this was nearly two decades before Disney/Pixar stole this idea and turned it into the animated hit movie *Inside Out*.

But the show, contrary to its title, also took place in the so-called real world, outside of Herman's head. This is where we get all of Herman's friends and colleagues. Those that are not mere abstract constructs brought to life in a cluttered attic setting. Those that are mere sitcom archetypes instead. There is the aforementioned Hank Azaria cocky character, Jay Nichols. Jay is Herman's best friend, and at times, his worst enemy. Jay is your typical arrogant womanizing alpha male character, who just as often fails at getting the girl, as he does at succeeding in bedding them. Of course, the always great Azaria would go on to a movie career in such films as *The Birdcage*, *Mystery Men*, *Along Came Polly*, and that classic work of cinema, *The Smurfs*. Over on *The*

Simpsons, he was the voice of pretty much half of the town of Springfield.

Next up is Heddy Newman, a fellow fact checker played by Jane Sibbett, who would go on to play Carol, Ross' ex-wife-turned-lesbian on *Friends*. Heddy is vicious and power-hungry, and takes every chance to put down Herman. Then there is Louise Fitzer, the office secretary. Played by Yeardley Smith, Louise is sweet and diminutive but also quite sassy a character. She acts as Herman's outside world conscious. In an increasing deepening of the characters as the show progressed, Louise will also find herself in an on again off again relationship with Jay throughout the second and third seasons of the show. This is a fun sidenote, as both actors were also working together on *The Simpsons* at the time, Smith as the voice of Lisa Simpson, and Azaria as various voices, such as Apu, Moe, and Comic Book Guy (aka, the aforementioned half of Springfield). In fact, both shows referenced each other on several occasions, including when Louise is told she sounds like Lisa Simpson.

The show also featured Jason Bernard as Mr. Bracken, the head of the fact checking department, who himself is a veritable fount of facts and trivia, and Edward Winter (Col. Flagg from *M*A*S*H*) as Mr. Crawford, an icy executive at the publishing firm. The show also had a penchant for old time TV stars, as both Bob Denver and Dawn Wells show up playing Gilligan and Mary Ann. Jennifer Aniston, not yet a TV star (*Friends* would start up two years after she first appeared here) also had a recurring part, as Herman's little sister in two episodes. These days, *Herman's Head* is probably a bit less forgotten than most of the shows in this book. At least I know most of my friends remember the show, and remember it fondly.

Woops! (1992)

Have you ever thought to yourself that there just haven't been enough situation comedies about the apocalypse? No good comedies about nuclear holocaust? Yeah, me too. But hey, back in the Fall of 1992, Fox decided to try their hand at just that very thing. And yes, it was a disaster. As much of a disaster as an actual nuclear holocaust? Probably not, but it did come rather close. Seriously, this is easily one of the worst shows in this entire book. An intriguing premise, yes, but an awful thing in reality. But hey, we're not here to merely bash a bad show, a show that is not around to defend itself, but to discuss said show. And perhaps learn a thing or two. So, let's get on with that, shall we?

The premise, as alluded to in the opening paragraph, is quite simple. Apparently, as is explained in the first episode, two kids are playing with a remote control car during a military parade, and accidentally launch a nuclear warhead. This accidental nuke bombing causes all other nuclear power countries to launch their warheads and missiles in retaliation. And then, boom! The world is over, and everything and everyone is destroyed. Well, not everything, as a lone farmhouse survives the eve of destruction. And not everyone either, as six survivors come out of the dust, and manage to find each other at this very farmhouse. Convenient, eh? Putting aside the massive implausibility of how this destruction happened, and the equal implausibility of these six survivors, all looking no worse for the wear mind you, stumbling across the lone surviving building, *Woops!* plays out a lot like *Gilligan's Island*. This could have been a fun way to go about things. Granted, when it comes to smartly written sitcoms, *Gilligan's Island* is no *Seinfeld*, but the show had a certain charm to it. *Woops!* however, has no charm whatsoever, and missed every opportunity to play on the riffs of Gilligan and his fellow castaways. Of course, *Woops!* had only 10 episodes to try and make this happen. Thirteen, if you count the final three episodes which never aired. Then again, the show was godawful bad from moment one. But again, enough bashing. Let's move on.

As for these six aforementioned survivors, they are each, much like in *Gilligan's Island*, a predictable archetype. We have Curtis Thorpe (Lane Davies), a former venture capitalist, who never takes off his suit and tie, even now that the world has ended; Suzanne Skillman (Marita Geraghty), your typical dumb blonde type, but for an added twist, a brunette; Frederick Ross (Cleavant Derricks), a doctor, as well as the apocalypse's only surviving person of color; Jack Conners (Fred Applegate), a former homeless man with an annoyingly sunny disposition; Alice McConell (Meagen Fay), the group's resident feminist; and Mark Braddock (Evan Handler), the show's lead, and, like many other show leads in TV history, the only character without some sort of stereotypical sitcom quirk. Think Judd Hirsch in *Taxi*, or Jerry in *Seinfeld*. So basically we have the cast of *Gilligan's Island*. Suzanne is Ginger, Alice is Mary Ann, Frederick is the Professor, Thorpe acts as both of the Howells, Jack is Gilligan, and Mark, although the lead, is the Skipper (still in charge). There are other similarities, such as wearing the same outfit day after day (were all clothes destroyed as well?) and ridiculous plot points (giant mutant turkeys and spiders, a crystal that makes Alice's breast grow, a visit from Santa in their somewhat early Christmas episode), but it is the isolation that is the major similarity. Every episode is a bottle episode. Too bad the producers and writers could not make it all work.

And speaking of the show's producers, they were Paul Junger Witt and Tony Thomas. This duo is responsible for such hit TV shows as *The Partridge Family, Soap, Benson*, and *The Golden Girls*. With *Woops!*, they missed the mark...by a lot. A whole lot. But, I suppose they can't all be hits. Heck, even Norman Lear made *a.k.a. Pablo* and *The Dumplings*. Anyway, the show only lasted a few months, and has been mostly forgotten since these few short months, hence its inclusion in this book. Most of the cast has also been forgotten. The only one to make a significant mark in pop culture, is Evan Handler, who was once Charlotte's hubby on *Sex and the City*, and more recently, Hank Moody's bumbling agent on *Californication*. Other than that, there is not much to mark this show in TV history, save for maybe a "worst of" list or two...or forty seven.

The Chevy Chase Show (1993)
The Magic Hour (1998)

I believe it was Andy Warhol who once said, "In the future, everyone will have a talk show for 15 minutes." Okay, maybe that's a bit of a misquote, but such a misquote is rather apropos for the two shows we will be discussing in this chapter. I'm sure anyone and everyone reading this book, has watched, or at least heard of the bigger names in the so-called Late Night Wars. Johnny Carson on the Tonight Show, David Letterman doing his own thing, Carson's rather lackluster replacement, Jay Leno. I'll betchya some of you even remember Arsenio Hall from back in the day. Now, of course, we have Jimmy Fallon at *The Tonight Show*, as well as Seth Myers, Stephen Colbert, James Corden, & Jimmy Kimmel. Even Arsenio came back for a while. But there have been others. Forgettable others. Sometimes rightfully forgettable others. But not to worry late night enthusiasts, for I am here to remind you of two of these rightfully forgotten late night talk shows. Perhaps two of the worst.

The names are most likely not forgotten, but their short-lived talk show travesties certainly are. The first up was *SNL* alum and (kinda) movie star, Chevy Chase. On September 7, 1993, *The Chevy Chase Show* premiered on Fox. It was the first attempt at late night talk on the young upstart network since *The Late Show Starring Joan Rivers* ran for two seasons from 1986 to 1988, which, incidentally, was the first ever program aired on the Fox Network. Maybe we should just ignore the fact that Fox's first choice for hosting their *Tonight Show* competitor was Dolly Parton, and move on. One thing that did not move on was Chase's show. Barely a month after it's debut, on October 17, 1993, Fox announced the show was cancelled. Chase, was great at sketch comedy, he even won three Emmys for it, but was not suited for the talk show circuit. Even his rather lame attempt at bringing back his *SNL* days with a "News Update" segment, bombed night after night. Time Magazine panned the show, saying "Nervous and totally at sea, Chase tried everything, succeeded at nothing." If only Dolly hadn't said no.

Then, five years after Chevy's fiasco, came an even worse mess of a late night talk show. *The Magic Hour*, which ran in syndication, was hosted by NBA legend and Hall of Famer, Earvin "Magic" Johnson. Just when America got the lingering foul taste of *The Chevy Chase Show* out of their collective mouths, came an even worse tasting attempt at talk showing. Don't get me wrong, Magic Johnson was one of the greatest basketball players of all time. Five time NBA champion, three time MVP, twelve time All-Star. A true GOAT. But, even moreso than the hapless Chase, Johnson was certainly no talk show host. Not even close. His show did last a bit longer though, as he was cancelled eight weeks after debuting, a whole two weeks longer than Chase. The sketch comedy show *MADtv* even made a recurring sketch about Johnson's ineptness at hosting a show. This recurring sketch was better than anything Johnson (or Chase) ever did on their shows. Trust me when I say these shows are rightfully forgotten. Sorry I had to remind you of them.

George (1993-94)
Emeril (2001)

Historically speaking, the best situation comedies are the ones with a strong comic presence at it's center. From Lucille Ball to Danny Thomas to Dick Van Dyke to Bob Newhart to Mary Tyler Moore to Rosanne Barr to Jerry Seinfeld and so on and so on and so on. This is the way you create a great comedy TV show. This is the way it is done. There is another way though. One where you take a person who has no right or reason being the star of any situation comedy. Perhaps a former heavyweight champion. Maybe a celebrity chef. Who needs someone with comedic or acting prowess when you have someone who has no business helming a hit comedy? Luckily, thanks to the general godawfulness of both shows, neither *George* nor *Emeril* ever had to worry about being a hit comedy.

Now don't get me wrong, just like Chevy and Magic in the last chapter, these were talented individuals. George Foreman was a hell of a boxer. A two-time world heavyweight champion and an Olympic gold medalist to boot. Emeril Lagasse is a great chef. A genius in the kitchen and the perfect person to host a cooking show. But the star of their own sitcom? I'm not saying someone outside of the comedy world cannot be funny. Just look at someone like The Rock who has great comic timing, even though he started out as a professional wrestler. He can be funny. But George Foreman and Emeril Lagasse? Neither of these men is particularly funny. Neither of these men could ever hold their own as the star of a situation comedy, even when they were both pretty much playing themselves. Luckily, thanks to the general godawfulness of both shows, neither *George* nor *Emeril* lasted long enough for their inability to lead a situation comedy to ever become a problem.

As for the shows themselves, both of which lasted just a mere ten episodes (not all of which actually made it onto the air) there isn't much to speak of. George Foreman played an ex boxer who helped children and Emeril Lagasse played himself, a la *Seinfeld*. Neither show is particularly good, and neither "actor" is particularly funny, which again is made even worse by the fact they were pretty much playing themselves. *George*, which aired on ABC, was produced by Tony Danza, fresh off of *Who's the*

Boss. Emeril, which aired on NBC (after being turned down by both ABC and CBS), was created and produced by Linda Bloodworth-Thomason, the woman responsible for *Designing Women*. So the pedigree was there on both shows. The comedy sadly, was not. Luckily, thanks to the general godawfulness of both shows, neither *George* nor *Emeril* were ever seen by enough people for it to even matter.

The Naked Truth (1995-98)

In the Fall of 1995, ABC placed a new show on Wednesday nights at 9:30. It was called *The Naked Truth*, and it was good. Perhaps not great, but still quite good. And what made this new situation comedy so good? That would be it's star, Tea Leoni. Coming off a 22 episode run in the failed sitcom *Flying Blind*, Leoni took on the role of Nora Wilde, a Pulitzer Prize nominated photographer, who was recently divorced from her multi-millionaire husband, stupidly refusing any money, and has now been blackballed from any legitimate job. That puts Nora on the doorstep of The Comet, a trashy tabloid run by Camilla Dane, who in turn is portrayed by the equally wonderful Holland Taylor. Leoni and Taylor play great off of each other, which works out spectacularly, because none of the supporting cast was even interesting enough to remember their names.

But no matter how well they played off of each other, the real surprise here is Tea Leoni. Let loose to be her weird and wacky self, something that the actress doesn't always get to do, and playing off the broad comedy surrounding a tabloid news rag, she ends up excelling in screwball comedy, and handed in week after week, some sort of gleeful Gilda Radner-esque antics. But not even Leoni's Gilda-esque antics, nor the way she and Taylor played off each other, nor even the handful of episodes that also featured a brilliantly over-the-top Tim Curry as the owner of The Comet, could save the show from being put on hiatus midway through the season, never to return to the network. Which is strange, since the show was no. 24 for the season, which is traditionally good enough to get renewed. Whatever the case, ABC let the series go – but that would not be the end of *The Naked Truth*.

A year later, coming on as a midseason replacement on NBC, *The Naked Truth* was back for a second season. But this time around, the show was a bit different. No longer revolving around the tabloid, which meant Taylor was now just a recurring character, the producers decided to showcase Nora and her private life more. Cheers alumni George Wendt joined the cast as the new owner of The Comet, Stupid Dave (Mark Roberts), who was named that because he was an idiot in the first season, was now just plain old Dave (probably realizing their mocking of a mentally challenged person was a bit un-PC), and Mary Tyler Moore and George Segal would make frequent guest appearances as Nora's parents. Gone were the zany antics of the first season. Also gone was the fun of the first season. On NBC, the show was merely an average sitcom about a working woman trying to find love. But it was also the 4th highest rated show of the season. Who knew? Take a fun show and make it average (not bad mind you, just mediocre) and the ratings go up.

Season three, still on NBC, saw Taylor's Camilla Dane move to a new tabloid, taking Nora along with her. Chris Elliott and Jim Rash were added to the cast. Gone was Amy Ryan, who played Nora's best friend in the first two seasons (with no mention of whatever became of her), and most of the staff of The Comet. Dave was still there though, and now not only was the stupid moniker gone, but so was his actual stupidity or mental disorder or whatever it was. Also gone were the ratings. Plummeting to 74th place in the Neilsens that year, NBC called it quits on the show. Leoni would go on to become a relatively big name star, and would end up starring as the Secretary of State for six seasons on CBS's hit political drama, *Madame Secretary*. Meanwhile, *The Naked Truth* would be mostly forgotten – and that's the truth.

Unhappily Ever After (1995-99)

Married... with Children was the breakout hit from the first season of Fox - it's initial 1987 attempt at competing with the big three networks of ABC, CBS, & NBC. It ran for eleven seasons, before finally coming to an end in 1997, the second longest running show ever on America's fourth network, and along with *The Simpsons* (Fox's longest running show) was an integral part in the rise of the upstart network, which eventually would allow Fox to realistically compete with the big three. Cut to January 11, 1995, and the birth of another upstart network, The WB. Starting out, as Fox had eight years prior, with just one night of original programming (Wednesday as opposed to Fox's original Sunday nights) The WB, the new television wing of Warner Bros. Entertainment, debuted four new situation comedies that night. One of these new shows, a bland comedy called *Muscle*, lasted thirteen episodes. The other three lasted five seasons each. *The Wayans Bros.*, featuring Shawn & Marlon Wayans, *The Parent*

'Hood, starring Robert Townsend, and *Unhappily Ever After*, which is the subject of this chapter, and The WB's biggest hope to follow the success of Fox's *Married... with Children*, and hopefully do for this upstart what that show did for that other upstart.

In fact, The WB was hoping for such a similar hit show, that they made the most similar show they could possibly make – without getting sued by Fox. Actually, *Unhappily Ever After*, which was so similar it was called *Divorced... with Children* by many industry insiders, was created by Ron Leavitt, who had also created, you guessed it, *Married... with Children*. Now there were some changes made. For example, no matter how much Peg and Al Bundy seemingly despised each other on Fox, they never got a divorce, and actually did love one another in their own weird ways. In contrast to this, the pilot for *Unhappily Ever After* has Jack Malloy being kicked out of his home by soon-to-be ex wife Jennie, and the show revolved around their separation, even after Jack is allowed to move back in, but only to live in the basement. Another difference is in the children. Instead of the older dumb daughter and younger smart son from the Bundy household, we get an older dumb son and a younger smart daughter in the Malloy household. Big difference, huh? They also even added a third child. Otherwise, this new WB show was a near carbon copy of the Fox show, especially in both show's fuck it attitudes.

But alas, even though it lasted five seasons, which means it had to have something going for it, *Unhappily Ever After* never became the cornerstone of The (new) WB. It was a mildly funny show, and Geoff Pierson was enjoyable as an Al Bundy retread, but Pierson and co-star Stephanie Hodge were certainly no Ed O'Neill and Katey Sagal. *Unhappily Ever After* did have one thing going for it that the other show did not. Mr. Floppy, a stuffed bunny that spoke to Jack, and was voiced by Bobcat Goldthwait. Yeah, the Bundys had a dog who talked to the camera on occasion, but that was it. Yes, The WB did have true hit series' later on (*Dawson's Creek, Charmed, Buffy the Vampire Slayer, Roswell, Smallville, Angel, 7th Heaven, Felicity,* and *Gilmore Girls*) but *Unhappily Ever After* was not the giant the upstart network was praying for. After it's cancellation, the show ran for a year in syndication, but due to low ratings, was cancelled from that as well.

As for the little upstart network, that ended in 2006, when their parent company closed down both The WB and former competitor UPN, which began as an upstart of its own a week after The WB, and created a new combined upstart called The

CW, which is still around today. Select programming from both networks moved over to the new upstart, most notably, *Supernatural*, which had it's debut season on The WB, before running another 14 years on The CW. Meanwhile, *Unhappily Ever After*'s default patriarch, Geoff Pierson, moved over to Fox, and onto *That 80's Show*, which can be found a few pages later in this very book, before becoming a regular on Showtime's smash hit *Dexter*. Oldest child Kevin Connolly moved onto the HBO series *Entourage*, and middle child Nikki Cox went onto her own WB sitcom, *Nikki* before moving to NBC and the hit dramedy *Las Vegas*, opposite Josh Duhamel. Meanwhile, over the years, *Unhappily Ever After* fell from most people's memories; hence it's insertion in this book.

<u>Sports Night</u> (1998-2000)

Some of the shows in this book were once big hits but sadly didn't travel well over the years. Some of the shows in this book deserve to be forgotten. And then there are those shows who were just ahead of their time. Shows that were good, even great, and once in awhile, downright brilliant, but just never caught on for one reason or another. *Sports Night*, which ran for just two seasons on ABC form 1998 to 2000, was one of these shows. Good, great, downright brilliant. And how could it not be, when it was created by Aaron Sorkin, the man responsible for *The West Wing*, one of the best damn TV shows to ever exist, not to mention writing such hit movies as *A Few Good Men* (adapted from his own stage play), *The American President*, *Moneyball*, and *The Social Network*, which won the guy an Oscar.

Sports Night was the story of a fictional television sports show called, of course, *Sports Night*. It starred Josh Charles of *Dead Poet's Society*, and later of *The Good Wife* on CBS, and Peter Krause, who would later star in HBO's *Six Feet Under* and NBC's

Parenthood, as co-anchors of the show within a show. Emmy Award winner Robert Guillaume of *Soap* and *Benson* fame, was the managing editor Isaac Jaffe. Future Emmy Award winner Felicity Huffman played executive producer Dana Whitaker, and Sabrina Lloyd was senior associate producer Natalie Hurley. William H. Macy, Huffman's hubby at the time, appeared frequently on the show as well, mostly as a foil to his wife's uptight character. The show was more than loosely based on the *ESPN SportsCenter* team of Keith Olbermann & Dan Patrick.

Sorkin wanted to create something that was part comedy and part drama – a dramedy if you will – and insisted on having no laugh track. ABC insisted otherwise, and since they were the money people, their insistence was louder and hence won out. Sorkin did manage to downplay the laugh track though, slowly fading it out throughout season one, and eliminating it completely by season two. This may have partly led to audience's indifference to the show, as it would still be a few years before it being a normal thing to exclude the antiquated idea of a laugh track. Although the show was smartly written and sharply acted by everyone on board (inter-character chemistry was through the roof), and even won itself a few Emmys (though never saw a well deserved Outstanding Comedy Series nomination in it's brief run), and had seemingly everything going for it, it just never caught on with audiences, and ABC cancelled it after just two seasons. After this premature cancellation, both HBO and Showtime (and other networks) made attempts at picking up the show for a third (or more) season, but Sorkin decided to let the show go in order to concentrate more on his other new show, *The West Wing* – a show that incorporated many of Sorkin's *Sports Night* attributes. *The West Wing*, of course, became a huge hit, and is still considered to be one of the finest shows in television history. The somewhat forgotten *Sports Night* though? No less a quality show, just a bit ahead of it's time.

The Secret Diary of Desmond Pfeiffer (1998)

Running for a mere four episodes on UPN in October of 1998, *The Secret Diary of Desmond Pfeiffer* manages to be one of the bigger failures in a book chock full of failures. And let's face it, the show probably deserves to be one of the bigger failures in a book chock full of failures. The story of Desmond Pfieffer (the P is pronounced), a black English nobleman who is chased out of England due to gambling debts, and somehow becomes valet to President Abraham Lincoln, had the distinct possibility of being seen as racist. Would it have a too light hearted take on slavery? Would it be a stereotypical stab at people of color? Would it be mere exploitation? In spite of protests from the NAACP before the premiere of the show, it was actually none of these things. It also wasn't very funny.

Coming off a regular gig on the critical hit *The John Larroquette Show*, Chi McBride starred as the titular nobleman turned valet. The role of our 16th President was played by Dann Florek, between his stints as Captain Donald Cragen on *Law & Order* and Captain Donald Cragen on *Law & Order: Special Victims Unit*. As opposed to the worry over the show's possible racist overtones, Pfieffer, the lone black man on the show, is actually the only intelligent person in a White House populated by drunkards and crooks and downright imbeciles. This reverse stereotyping doesn't change the fact that the show just wasn't very funny. In fact it was so unfunny that it didn't even last a month on the air before being pulled. Five episodes went unaired, but they would not have helped. In the end, *The Secret Diary of Desmond Pfieffer*, has stayed one of the best kept secrets in television history – and that is probably a very good thing.

Action (1999)

Perhaps the reason that *Action* lasted only eight episodes on Fox, had nothing to do with the quality of the show itself. In fact, if I can act as a harbinger of taste for just a moment, this could not possibly be the reason. The show was deftly written, smartly acted, and a downright pleasure to watch. Granted, it was a rather acerbic, biting pleasure, but a pleasure nonetheless. No, a lack of quality could not have been the reason. Trust me, I have seen many a television show be torn off the air for lack of quality. These shows are in undue abundance, a dime a dozen, if you will, all throughout television history, and all throughout the pages of this book. And this is not just me talking here, for the show was more than critically acclaimed while it aired for those eight weeks back in the Fall of 1999. No, the reason must be something else, and the best idea this critic can come up with, and perhaps the easiest as well, is that it was just ahead of its time. I know, I've said that of at least half a dozen other shows in this book already, but I'm saying it again here and now. That's my story and I'm sticking with it.

Action was created by Chris Thompson, creator of the cross-dressing comedy *Bosom Buddies*, which gave Tom Hanks his big break, and the tabloid satire sitcom, *The Naked Truth* (another forgotten gem to be found in this very book). This sly show revolved around the unscrupulous movie producer Peter Dragon, played brilliantly by *SNL* alum, Jay Mohr, who is in desperate need of a hit movie to keep his career and his company, Dragonfire Films, going. The great and sexy indie film character actress Illeana Douglas, best known for her roles in then boyfriend Martin Scorsese's films, co-starred as former child star Wendy Ward, who lost her stardom due to a teen coke addiction before becoming a high priced call girl, and then later Vice President of Production at Dragonfire Films. The show also featured the legendary Buddy Hackett in one of his final roles.

Even though there were quite a few celebrity cameos, such as Keanu Reeves, Salma Hayek, and David Hasselhoff, the show took scathing stabs at the culture of Hollywood and all those working in it. Perhaps this blatant attack on the so-called hand that feeds you was an integral cog in the reasons why *Action* only lasted eight lousy episodes before having it's proverbial plug pulled. The remaining five episodes that went unaired on Fox, later found their way onto the air via channels like Comedy Central. It is a real crying shame that this one is not better remembered.

Two Guys, a Girl and a Pizza Place (1998-2001)

The story is simple. This ABC sitcom that ran for four seasons, was about two guys, a girl, and a pizza place. Well, at least for the first two seasons. In season three, in order to streamline the show, the pizza place was dropped as a setting, and from the title (now just known as *Two Guys and a Girl*). But the basic premise stayed the same throughout. Three friends, a girl and two guys (duh) who go to Tufts University. Sharon (the girl of the title) was played by Traylor Howard, who had just come off of the even less remembered sitcom *Boston Commons*, and who would eventually become the assistant to Tony Shalhoub's *Monk*. Richard Ruccolo played Peter (one of the two guys) while Berg (the other guy) was played by the still-unknown Ryan Reynolds, years before he would become the psychopathic anti-hero Deadpool, and a general all-around movie star.

The show revolved around the wacky antics of these characters as they struggled to make it through college, and post pizza place, the real world that came after college. Sharon was the sensible one. Peter the neurotic one, and Berg the troublemaker. The show also featured Nathan Fillion, just before becoming Captain Mal on the short-lived but far from forgotten *Firefly*. Overall, the show was rather tired, with only Reynolds stepping up to truly entertain. But that didn't stop it's success. The ratings were solid at first. It's pilot episode was the biggest pilot ABC had in years, and though it could only go down from there, the ratings stayed relatively good (emphasis on the word relatively) throughout it's first three seasons, managing 36th, 44th, and 57th places while it was on Wednesday nights. ABC's fourth season decision to move the show to Friday nights, opposite ratings giant *Who Wants to Be a Millionaire*, was it's death knell. The show dropped to 104th place, and eventual cancellation. In the final episode, fans were polled to decide what happened to each of the characters. I would tell you what happened to them, but to be honest, I forget. Or maybe I just don't care. Take your pick.

<u>Normal, Ohio</u> (2000-01)

As modern society has progressed, or at least tried to progress, so has television. In the past twenty years or so, there have been several TV shows which have shown the LGBTQ community in a positive light. Most notably are the comedies *Will & Grace*, *Modern Family* and *Schitt's Creek*, Showtime dramas, *Queer as Folk* and *The L Word*, and the high school musical, *Glee*. Other shows, such as *Roseanne, Dawson's Creek, Melrose Place,* and *My So-Called Life*, have also delved positively into this once taboo TV subject matter. These shows, for the most part, take away the prejudice, the stereotypes, and the antiquated thinking on such matters, and instead give us laughter, love, and honest, warts and all, portrayals of those in the LGBTQ community. *Normal, Ohio* is not one of these shows.

This is not to say that Fox's 2000 sitcom took any sort of derogatory spin on the idea of equal rights. In fact, just the opposite. The premise of *Normal, Ohio* was one layered around the normality of homosexuality. An attempt at showing how homosexuality is no different than heterosexuality. Trying to show how both sides of this so-called coin, this often controversial subject matter, are truly one and the same. Now, in a perfect world, this would be a no-brainer. People are people, love is love, and all that, but unfortunately we do not live in that perfect world, and there are still a great many people who harbor some level of homophobia. In *Normal, Ohio*, we are given John Goodman, the gentle giant of the blue collar world of *Roseanne*, as Butch Gamble (yeah, Butch), an openly gay man, who after twenty years of marriage, drops the out-of-the-closet bombshell on his family, and heads to California to find himself.

In the pilot episode, we are introduced to Butch as he comes back home after four years.

Now I realize the whole idea in casting Goodman in the lead role, was to show that gay men did not have to be the flamboyant queens we so often see in movies and on TV. Gay men could also be football loving, beer guzzling, big lovable bears as well. Now, of course, this is true, there are all different kinds of gay men, just like there are all different types of straight men, but even so, Goodman just never seems to ring all that true in the role. Basically we are watching his Dan Conner character (they even share the same occupation of contractor), just three years after *Roseanne* left the air, seemingly coming out of the closet. Was the American viewing public ready for such a thing back in 2000? It may not seem all that long ago, but in terms of how far gay and lesbian rights have come since then, it might as well be a lifetime. But even beyond what the typical American audience thought of the show, when one takes a closer look, was the show really as progressive as we are led to believe? Probably not.

Yes, *Normal, Ohio* took the stereotypical gay man, and tossed him on his preconceived head. Sure, Goodman's sturdy Midwestern stock of a man was a far cry from the flamers typically portrayed in our media. But really, doesn't he still end up as just another gay joke? In the few episodes we were given (just 12 episodes were made, of which only 8 aired before cancellation) Butch's butch persona is interspersed with bits of stereotypical flourishes. Happily singing a few bars from The Trolley Song or references to *The Wizard of Oz* or the occasional snarky effeminate comeback. The audience is free to laugh at these pinches of typical "gayness," and we are also free to laugh at the obvious disgust that Orson Bean, as Butch's homophobic, but with a heart of gold somewhere in there, old man, shows for his son. With labels such as fruit loop or gone fluffy, Butch's dad gruffs at the son he feels he has lost. Yeah, in the end, we see that he does love his son, no matter what, but the gay-baiting is still there. Was this intentional? Probably not, but it is still there.

The show was created by husband & wife *SNL* alums, Bonnie Turner and Terry Turner, who already had a pair of hits with *3rd Rock from the Sun* and *That 70's Show*. Their casting Goodman, as the atypical gay man, in the lead role was both what could have made the show work and what kept the show from working. To answer my own question from a few paragraphs back, no, I do not think 2000 American audiences were ready for this kind of performance from this kind of actor. More recently, TV has given us Cameron on *Modern Family*, played brilliantly by Eric Stonestreet. Cameron is also an atypical gay man, in that he is a rabid sports fan (TV really needs to get past such a stereotype), but at the same time, he is given to theatrical flourishes that would make Liberace blush. This seems to be more acceptable, safer even, to the typical American television viewer, even in 2020, when these words are being written. Perhaps *Normal, Ohio* just came along too soon. Or perhaps the show just wasn't all that good, forward thinking or not.

The show actually didn't revolve around Butch's homosexuality as much as one would think. In most episodes, we don't see a show about a gay man, so much as a show which happens to have a gay man in it. Now that is progressive. Much like what Dan Levy did with *Schitt's Creek*. Making the idea of sexuality or gender identification a moot point. But still, unlike the hilarious *Schitt's Creek,* the show was only moderately funny. The writing was average at best, and the show as a whole, followed suit down that very middle-of-the-road mentality. The highlight of most episodes, were the manic antics of Joely Fisher, known mostly at this time, as Ellen DeGeneres' BFF on the comic's self-titled hit sitcom of the 90's. Fisher plays Pamela, Butch's usually frazzled single mom of a sister. Butch may have been the one to break his parent's hearts when he came out in his forties, but it is Pamela who is the biggest disappointment in the family, and Fisher plays it perfectly. Sadly though, the so-called highlights of *Normal, Ohio* end right about there. Today, if one were so interested, one could find all 12 episodes of *Normal, Ohio*, steaming online somewhere. As for being an important piece in bringing middle America closer to an understanding of the LGBTQ community, the show never lasted long enough for any of us to find out.

The Michael Richards Show (2000)
Bob Patterson (2001)
Watching Ellie (2002-03)

For nine seasons, from 1989 to 1998, *Seinfeld* was both a ratings champ and a critical darling, and even today, nearly 20 years after leaving the air, it is still considered one of the best TV shows of all time. It sits atop many a list for the best comedies on TV, including my own. The show put Jerry Seinfeld, Jason

Alexander, Julia Louis-Dreyfus, and Michael Richards on the pop culture map. Still to this day, sayings like "No soup for you!," and "Master of your domain," are batted back and forth all over the place. There really was no reason for these four household names to have trouble moving on post *Seinfeld*. Well, unless you take into consideration the power of the *Seinfeld* Curse. Yes, I said curse. Granted, Jerry himself never really attempted to follow his show up. The stand up went directly back on the road, doing what he did best. The others though? There were some really sad attempts at post-Seinfeld careers.

The first of these attempts was *The Michael Richards Show*, which premiered on October 24, 2000 and bowed out eight episodes later on December 19th. The show revolved around Richards being an inept private eye. Even with several of the writers from *Seinfeld* aboard, Richards could not make the show work. Strike one. Next up was Jason Alexander as Bob Patterson in...well, in *Bob Patterson*. This show, which revolved around Alexander being a motivational speaker, topped his old co-star's record and was cancelled after just five episodes. The show ran from October 2, 2001 to October 31st. He couldn't even get past the first month. Five episodes went unaired. Strike two. Then in 2002 came *Watching Ellie*.

At first, *Watching Ellie*, starring Julia Louise-Dreyfus, and created by her husband, Brad Hall, looked like it might actually break that old *Seinfeld* curse. But alas, it did not. It did manage to last longer than the others, actually making it to a second season. But it's not as successful as that makes it sound. The show focused on Ellie, a cabaret singer. At first the show was done with a single camera and was filmed in real time, showing a 22 minute slice of Ellie's day. There was even a countdown clock in the corner of the screen. This failed rather dismally, with only ten episodes aired. But not to fret, as the show was somehow given a second season, but only with the stipulation that it be reformatted. So, season two saw a more traditional multi-camera set-up. This too was a dismal failure, and was cancelled after just six episodes. Strike three. Jason Alexander did have a second failed sitcom, but I think we've embarrassed him enough already. Plus, there is no strike four in this game.

But then one magical day, the curse was lifted. Hallelujah! The date was August 27, 2006. As Julia Louis-Dreyfus picked up her Emmy Award for Outstanding Actress in a Comedy Series, for the first season of her new sitcom, *The New Adventures of Old Christine*, she held the golden statuette above her head and said "I'm not somebody who really believes in curses, but curse this, baby!" Julia Louis-Dreyfus would go on to win six more Best Actress Emmys for yet another hit show, *Veep*, on HBO. Combine these with the Emmy she had already won for *Seinfeld*, and not only does that tie her with Cloris Leachman for the most Emmy acting awards, it also makes her the only performer to nab an Emmy for three different starring roles on three different TV shows. Jason Alexander and Michael Richards? Well, they're still waiting to beat that damned curse.

That 80's Show (2002)

Even though it was created and produced by many of the same people as the successful and fondly remembered *That 70's Show*, and is pretty much the exact same set-up, only eight or so years later, the similarly titled *That 80's Show* was never successful, and is not all that remembered. The failure of this show, created basically just to ride the wave of popularity kicked up by *That 70's Show*, probably has a lot to do with it being a mere cheap copy of a superior show. While *That 70's Show* had in depth storylines and multifaceted characters who grew as people, *That 80's Show* seemed more like a show that was just there to product placement everything from the Rubik's Cube to *Dynasty* drinking games. The characters and story were merely background noise for jokes about 80's hair styles and shoebox-sized mobile phones, while in *That 70's Show*, the decade and its own era appropriate pop culture references were background for the stories and characters. This is probably why one show lasted 8 seasons and 200 episodes, and still lives on in syndication, while the other didn't make it past 4 months and 13 episodes.

But let's not hate on this show too much. It did have its moments during its 13 episode run in the Spring of 2002. Not many, but a few, which is more than can be said for some of the shows in this book. The show was set in 1984 San Diego, and revolved around struggling musician and record store employee, Corey Howard, and his friends and family. Corey was played by Glenn Howerton, who three years after *That 80's Show* was canceled, would help create and develop, as well as star in, the FX series, *It's Always Sunny in Philadelphia*, which is still on the air as of the writing of this book – and incidentally, about to become the longest running live action comedy ever to be in prime time. Supposedly, Corey was the cousin of Topher Grace's Eric Forman from *That 70's Show*, which technically makes this a spin-off series, though in the most flexible meaning of the term. Perhaps if some of *That 70's Show* characters had transcended time, and made an appearance or two on this show, things would have turned out better for *That 80's Show*. Then again, perhaps not.

As I said, the show revolved around Glenn Howerton's Corey. splitting its time between his home life and his work life. At home we have R.T., Corey's divorced and bitter dad, played by veteran actor Geoff Pierson, Pierson is known for recurring roles on such shows as *Dexter, 24,* and *Boardwalk Empire*, as well as the daytime soap, *Ryan's Hope*. Pierson also starred in the 1990's WB series, *Unhappily Ever After*, which in much the same way this show was cashing in on the success of *That 70's Show*, was created to cash in on the success of *Married with Children* (see a few chapters back). But, if you have been reading this book in chronological order, you already know that story, as it was covered a few chapters back. R.T. is the vain, relatively wealthy owner of a personal fitness company called Videx, that produces Thigh Master-esque products such as the Gut Wacker and the Butt Luge. R.T., along with Corey's best bud Roger, played by Eddie Shin, represent the monetary excess of the 1980's. R.T. has such excess, while Roger, living above the Howard's garage, like a latter day wannabe Fonzie, wants it desperately.

Also at home is Corey's naive but syrupy sweet Valley Girl sister, Katie. Played by Tinsley Grimes, Katie is a bubbly college drop-out and budding environmentalist, who is counted on by her father to be the caretaker around the house. Meanwhile, Corey's ex girlfriend, Sophia (Brittany Daniel, a one-time Doublemint Twin), has announced she is bi-sexual, and that she has a huge crush on Katie. Much of Sophia's time on the show, when not showcasing her shallow archetypal 1980's party girl personality, is based around her *Three's Company*-esque attempts at getting into Katie's ruffled polka dot skirts and pastel colored, shoulder-padded jackets. Eventually, Sophia becomes the power-hungry, cut-throat director of marketing at Videx, and moves into the Howard home. We also get to see the occasional Owen, Katie's Navy boyfriend, but not all that much, so there's nothing really interesting to say about him.

When not at his pastel-painted home, or at Club Berlin, the appropriately 80's era dance club highlighted in many episodes, Corey is at work. This work is a record store, back when there were still record stores, called Permanent Record. With an attitude somewhere in between *High Fidelity* and *Empire Records*, Permanent Record is an adorably indie hole-in-the-wall shop run by ex-hippie Margaret, played by stand-up comic Margaret Smith. Smith, who has won six Emmy Awards for writing *The Ellen DeGeneres Show*, brings her wry, deadpan stage persona to the role of the sardonic record shop owner. She is often shown either berating a customer for their bad taste in music or reminiscing about all the rock stars she has slept with. But the biggest deal over at Permanent Record is the Sam & Diane, Ross & Rachel back and forth between Corey and fellow record store employee, Tuesday. Played by Chyler Leigh, who would go on to star in *Grey's Anatomy*, Tuesday is a jaded punk rocker, complete with liberty spikes and bad attitude.

The sexual tension is obvious from the moment we first meet Corey and Tuesday, and any regular sitcom watcher knows from this very moment, exactly where everything is going. Sure, after several episodes of bantering insults back and forth, Corey and Tuesday do finally go exactly where we all knew they would. Yes, it's cliché, and beyond obvious, and has been done to death in about a million sitcoms before, but Howerton and Leigh still make it work here. In the end though, we never do find out what happens with Corey and Tuesday beyond the thirteen episodes, or any of the characters really.

Yes, Katie ends up going back to school, and the party boy Roger even gets himself a regular girlfriend before the show's end. This new girl, only in a few episodes, was played, hysterically mind you, by Tammy Lynn Michaels, also known in real life as Mrs. Melissa Etheridge. We also got a slew of 1980's-centric guest stars, from Debbie Gibson and Tiffany to Pat Benatar and Duran Duran's John Taylor, but overall, we were all left wanting, when the show was canceled in May of 2002. Okay, perhaps we weren't all left wanting, but those of us who actually liked the show back then (and contrary to some of my trash talk in the opening paragraph, I did actually like this show), or any of those who still remember it now...well okay, maybe that is not a very long list, but the show wasn't all that bad, just all that unsuccessful. And perhaps all that forgettable too.

Boy Meets Boy (2003)
Playing it Straight (2004)
Seriously, Dude, I'm Gay (2004)

In this more progressive day and age of tolerance, the idea of homosexuality, once considered both a mental disease and illegal, is much more accepted. Yes, the world still has homophobic people, just as it has racism and sexism, but it is a much brighter time than those pre-Stonewall days of hiding in the closet lest ye be stoned by an ignorant public. In my opinion, homosexuality, along with any other sexuality, from pansexual to polysexual to heterosexual, should not be a concern for anyone. What a fellow human being is, and what a fellow human being likes, should be of no concern of yours. We are people, not labels.

Of course this utopian mindset is far from reality, but it does seem as if we are slowly but surely getting to that utopian place. Even as recently as 15 or 20 years ago, the idea of people being gay or lesbian was a novelty to most of society. Whether it was the hardcore gay haters (a group that needs to be eradicated) or just those average Karens & Kyles who thought someone else's sexual identity was somewhat off putting but ultimately satisfied their own desire to be entertained. Just like people of color back in the day, being allowed on stage to entertain the white folks via music or dancing or what have you, but not being allowed to sit and dine or drink in those clubs, there was a time in American culture when people of the LGBTQ community were good enough to entertain the straight folks, but not good enough to be taken seriously. As I said, things are better, though still far from perfect these days, but just after the turn of the Millennium, things were still in that "Entertain Us" phase, and that is when we were given this trio of gay-themed reality TV minstrel shows.

The first to hit was Bravo's *Boy Meets Boy*, which ran on the cable channel for six weeks in the Summer of 2003. The basic premise was optimistic in it's seemingly progressive take. The show was a gay take on *The Bachelor*, an inexplicably popular dating reality series that had debuted just a year prior on ABC. James Getzlaff, a gay man, would sift through a stable of eligible bachelors in hopes of finding a real love connection. Well, as real as something can be on reality TV. But there was a kicker. A gay-man-as-joke twist. You see, the fifteen would be suitors on the show consisted of not only gay men also searching for a real love connection (again, as real as anything can be on reality TV), but several straight men "playing" gay. Our hapless hopeful James was not in on the joke, nor were the actual gay members of the cast. The audience knew though. At least part way through they knew. They were let in on the joke long before the contestants were. In the end, if James chose a fellow gay man as his real love connection, the two would win prize money and a trip for two to New Zealand. If poor James picked a straight man, he would get nothing, and the straight actor would walk away $25,000 richer. Truly gay for pay.

But this Bravo series was not the only potentially offensive reality show take on this subject. In the Spring of 2004, Fox joined the fray with their show, *Playing it Straight*. This time around, the roles were reversed, with a woman contestant trying to find that so-called real love connection amongst a group of straight men and gay men playing it straight. The end results were the same. Pick a straight guy and fly off into the sunset a million dollars richer, pick a gay man and get nothing while he flies off a million dollars richer. At least we are now getting equal opportunity fleecing of people's emotions. But alas, these shows were not the worst of this gaydar triumvirate. Not even close. Fox was planning something even more controversial, even more insulting than either of these shows had already given us. The show was called *Seriously, Dude, I'm Gay*. Well, it would have been called that if it ever made it onto television. Thanks to GLAAD, it never did.

You may ask yourself, what exactly was it that drew the ire of the Gay & Lesbian Alliance Against Defamation. What did this show potentially have that these other two offensive yet still somewhat palpable (at least palpable enough to not get GLAAD in a bunch over them) shows didn't have? This show had two straight male contestants face off against each other by having them play gay. The contestants had to convince their friends and families and co-workers that they were indeed gay. After this they would be judged by a panel of gay men, who just so happened were told that one of the contestants was gay and one was straight. This panel of gay men, billed in promos as "jury of their queers," decided who seemed the most gay. Although the network fought back with promises of the show being the champion of the LGBTQ community, with quotes from the straight contestants such as "worst nightmare" and "trapped in gay hell," they ended up acquiescing and dropping it from their planned June 7th telecast.

Personally, I am far from a fan of reality television, and think 90% of it is pure crap, but these three shows took it down to a whole other level of sludge. Luckily, these shows are long forgotten (one was never seen in the first place), but hopefully the lesson one can learn from them is not. We are growing ever closer to complete acceptance of people's sexuality and gender identification, and one the most important things in getting there is, not only eradicating aggressive homophobia from the playing field (which should be a given), but also eradicating the more passive forms of homophobia, like these gay minstrel shows, from seeing the light of day. Good riddance to 'em all.

Joey (2004-06)

Running for ten seasons, and garnering 62 Emmy nominations, the NBC sitcom *Friends* was one of the most successful, and most beloved series in television history. When the gang called it quits at the end of the 2003-04 TV season, not because of low ratings (it was the fourth most watched show in it's final year), but because they thought it was time to graciously bow out and move on, one of the six cast members wasn't quite ready to say goodbye. Matt LeBlanc, who played the dumb but loveable Joey Tribbiani for the past decade, wanted to stick around and keep enjoying the success the show offered. As hindsight is 20/20, Leblanc probably knows better now, but in the Summer of 2004, the actor playing an actor, began filming the only *Friends* spin-off to ever be.

This new show, titled simply, *Joey*, showed the character striking out on his own, and moving to sunny L.A. in order to further pursue his dream of becoming a famous actor. The show was created by Scott Silveri and Shana Goldberg-Meehan, both of whom were executive producers on *Friends*, and would marry in 2006. *Friends* creators Marta Kauffman and David Crane wanted nothing to do with the show, and handed it off to their co-executive producer on *Friends*, Kevin S. Bright. So, on September 9, 2004, *Joey* premiered in its predecessor's old timeslot, Thursday night at 8pm. This first show, just from it's pedigree alone, was a ratings winner. But it would only be downhill from there. Panned by both critics, and an audience looking for another *Friends*, the show's ratings, though good by any other standards throughout the first season, were still far from the *Friends*-esque juggernaut the network was hoping for. It did get renewed for a second season though – most likely due it's pedigree.

Along with LeBlanc's Joey, the show also featured his sister Gina, played by Drea de Matteo, who was fresh off the HBO drama *The Sopranos*, and who would win an Emmy for that show just a week and a half after *Joey* premiered. Gina, whose character had appeared on *Friends*, but was played by a different actress, was a promiscuous L.A. hairdresser, who wasn't all that much brighter than her baby brother. Gina had been living in L.A. with her twenty year old son, Michael. Michael, played by Paulo Costanzo, is a brilliant engineering student (an actual rocket scientist) who immediately moves in with his Uncle Joey in order to escape his domineering mother and learn how to talk to women. Adam Goldberg, who appeared on *Friends* as Chandler's short lived crazy roommate Eddie, who moved in when Joey moved out in season two, had a recurring role as Michael's father. The show also featured Andrea Anders as Alex, a corporate lawyer who also happens to be Joey's neighbor and landlady. After becoming friends, Alex and Joey become romantically involved. Anders and LeBlanc also became romantically involved in real life, and would go on to have nine year relationship. For more on Anders, check out the next show in this book.

In its second season, ratings were not as good, mostly due to NBC moving it from 8pm on Thursdays and placing it in the 8:30 spot on Tuesdays, forcing it to compete with the second half of ratings behemoth *American Idol*. After a not great but still respectable 35th place finish in year one, *Joey* came in 86th place in year two. In March, the network put the show on hiatus, and officially cancelled it on May 15, 2006. The remaining episodes never aired on NBC, but did show up in a few international broadcasts. This early cancellation was a shame, as the show really wasn't all that bad. Granted, it wasn't to the level of *Friends*, but it was still a funny show that may have lasted more than it's two seasons (or season and a half actually) if it was not constantly being compared to its predecessor. Even though it was a funny show (and di Matteo was brilliant as the trashy but loveable Gina), *Joey* never had the same feel as *Friends*, and the character of Joey never had the same feel either. Exec Producer Kevin S. Bright thought so too, saying "Joey was deconstructed to be a guy who couldn't get a job, couldn't ask a girl out. He became a pathetic, mopey character."

Just before *Friends*, LeBlanc had starred in back-to-back failed sitcoms, *Top of the Heap* in 1991 and *Vinnie & Bobby* in 1992-93. Both shows lasted 7 episodes each. Now, after his ten years as one of the most beloved characters on television, and another two as the same character, but not as beloved anymore, the actor took some time off before making a comeback in 2011 on the US-UK sitcom *Episodes*, where he played a fictionalized version of himself. LeBlanc was nominated for four consecutive Emmy Awards for the show, and won the Golden Globe for the part. Later, he was the host of the British car show series, *Top Gear*, before coming back to American television on *Man with a Plan*, which ran for four seasons on CBS.

<u>The Class</u> (2006-07)

For the 2006-07 TV season, CBS gave us a grade school reunion. The premise of the series pilot of *The Class*, goes as follows. Ethan Haas, played by Jason Ritter, son of sitcom legend John, plans a surprise party for his fiancée, Joanne Richman (Casey Wilson). Ethan decides that this surprise party needs to be populated by their third grade classmates, which is where the couple had originally met twenty years prior. So, Ethan tracks down seven of his classmates for a surprise party and 20th third grade class reunion. But alas, Joanne was already on the verge of leaving Ethan, so the party isn't the big hoopla he had hoped for. The rest of the season revolved around these eight old classmates getting to know each other again.

The cast was filled with all your typical archetypes. The naive and noble Ethan. The sweet and sour fraternal twins, Kat and Lina. The blonde trophy wife Nicole. The lovable lunkhead Duncan. The constant failure Richie. You get the idea. But standard sitcom types or not, the show was smartly written and well acted by all involved. In fact the show was almost a hit before it was even cast. David Crane, the man behind the creation of *Friends* (a show that definitely does not belong in this book) and his partner Jeffrey Klarik, who co-created *Episodes* with Crane (a show that sadly, may belong in this book) and was a producer on the hit series *Mad About You*, came up with the premise, and because of their successes, were courted by all the networks, finally deciding to go with CBS, before even a pilot was filmed. The ratings for the show were middling at best, only reaching the top 40 twice in their 19 episode run, peaking at #34 in their season finale. Overall, it came in 65th place for the season. This rating was more than enough (or less than enough, as it were) to get it cancelled on May 15, 2007. Although this final ranking was still three spots up from *The Office*, which would get renewed for a fourth season, of an eventual nine. But that was NBC's decision. CBS decided to go the other way with *The Class*. Its timeslot would be given to the new series, *The Big Bang Theory*, the following season. A show that, if people had any taste, would be a strong candidate for this book. But I digress.

As for the cast, most of them have gone on to relative obscurity. Star Jason Ritter would go on to do other shows, but never reaching the heights his father hit. Lizzy Kaplin, who played the sarcastic Kat was basically best known as the one time significant other of *Friends*' Matthew Perry. Andrea Anders, who portrayed popular Nicole, was basically best known as the one time significant other of *Friends*' Matt LeBlanc (they met while starring on the *Friends* spin-off, *Joey* – see last chapter). English actress Lucy Punch, who had been fired before season's end in order to cut costs and allow CBS to extend the season by six more episodes, would go on to appear in many shows and films, but as far as this author knows, was never romantically tied to any cast member of *Friends*. The show did spawn two TV success stories though. Jon Bernthal, the aforementioned loveable lunkhead Duncan, would go on to play antihero Shane on the first two seasons of *The Walking Dead*, and later as the antihero Frank Castle on Netflix's *The Punisher*. Meanwhile Jesse Tyler Ferguson would go on to co-star on *Modern Family* (another show that does not belong in this book) and garner five consecutive Primetime Emmy Award nominations (always a bridesmaid, never a bride). In the end there had been a fan campaign to try to get CBS to change their minds on the cancellation, but alas, said campaign did not work and the show fell into that forgotten zone that gave it a place in this book.

Cavemen (2007)

Let's make a TV sitcom! Sounds fun, doesn't it? But just how should one go about such a thing? Well, let's find out. Step one: take a series of witty 30 second commercials for an insurance company, and turn them into a half hour situation comedy. This idea is actually somewhat intriguing, and possibly rather daring as well. But would it ever work? Let's move on to the next step and find out - as if you haven't already figured out how this is all going to end. Let's see, I suppose step two should be something along the lines of making the whole shebang funny. The problem with ABC's *Cavemen*, based on a series of creative Geico Insurance ads, is that it is not funny. Not one damn bit. Not even one iota. One would think that they would have tried to make the show funny, and instead just simply failed at such an endeavor. Many shows have failed at such a thing. But with *Cavemen*, it's almost as if they were purposely trying to not make it funny. Now I know that such a thing could never be the case here, but it did seem this way when it all went down. It really did.

Seriously though, all hyperbole aside, this sitcom did have an interesting premise. Placing unevolved cavemen in with the rest of modern society could be mined for that so-called comedy gold. Yeah, it came from a TV commercial, but really, I do think under better circumstances, it could have been a smart and funny show. There was more than ample room for social satire here - a very promising premise indeed. Sadly enough though, this is one of the most unfunny shows I have ever seen. It's not that the thing was bad. At least not bad in the sense of *Joanie Loves Chachi* bad. It certainly wasn't *Small Wonder* bad. It definitely wasn't *Homeboys in Outer Space* bad. It wasn't bad so much as it was just boring. So damn boring. Granted, there are a handful of humorous moments in the six episodes which aired (another seven episodes went unaired after cancellation) but these moments are way too few and way too far between, for anyone's good. And to think, the series was the brainchild of Joe Lawson, who would go on to be a writer and producer on *Modern Family*, one of the best and wittiest sitcoms in television history. But as I've said before, they can't all be winners.

As I said, just a mere six episodes ever saw the proverbial light of day, running ever so briefly in October and November of 2007, and therefore were probably missed by most of the TV watching population. Granted, thanks to the popularity of the commercials, and some good marketing, the first episode drew a more than fair audience, and was actually number one in it's timeslot. After this, and after the critical thumping that followed the airing of this first episode, the show quickly dropped to last place in its time slot, and stayed there until its eventual and inevitable cancellation...a mere six weeks later. All to be totally forgotten as time marched on.

Though Lawson, who had created the ad campaign as well as the truncated TV show, did at least have some fun with the cancellation, and got in one last self-effacing jab. A new ad was made specially to air at the 2008 Super Bowl, with the commercial cavemen making fun of the TV show, with dialogue like, "What was the deal with that make-up?" "Exactly! Why not just use real cavemen?" I'm guessing, since this ad aired during the Super Bowl, that it had higher ratings than the show could have ever hoped to have. Yeah, that's right.

Overall, *Cavemen* suffered the same terrible fate as many an *SNL* sketch-turned-motion picture. Yeah, on *Saturday Night Live*, a five to seven minute sketch may be damn funny, but when one tries to stretch those five to seven minutes out to an hour and a half or more, we get things like *The Coneheads* movie or *A Night at the Roxbury*. Yeah, I know there are successes coming from *SNL* as well (*Blues Brothers, Wayne's World*) but these are the oh so vast minority. Most of these sketch-turned-movies, even the ones that are funny in short spurts, are disasters on the big screen. So, just like *Stuart Saves His Family* or *Ladies Man*, even though they were funny in sketch form, were just godawful in long form, these Geico cavemen were funny in their short commercial spots (at least I thought so), but in their half hour run...alas, not so much. And I haven't even mentioned the anger of the supposed blatant racism that many said accompanied the never-aired pilot episode, with the cavemen being used as cheap metaphor for the African American in modern society.

After the acidic responses of test audiences, the writers and producers were forced to go rushing back into the studio, to change the show enough, including a setting change from Atlanta to the more racially antiseptic San Diego, for their actual TV debut just a few weeks later. The ironic thing about this development was that this un-aired pilot, though still mostly unfunny, was not racist, but rather took a stab at society's racist attitudes, and came closer to the intended satire of the show, and was actually far better than any of the episodes that actually aired.

ABC actually had the audacity to promote the show with the tagline, "A unique buddy comedy that offers a clever twist on stereotypes and turns race relations on its head." If only the show had gone this deep. Or even if the show had seemed to actually try to do so. The dark comedy that comes with the so-called clever twist promised in the aforementioned tagline, could have been that oh so elusive comedy gold we all had wished for. Instead we got what some called base race baiting (intentional or not) in the pilot episode, followed by six episodes of pure mediocrity, followed by another six episodes, which only aired in Australia. Why in Australia, I honestly do not know. All I do know for sure is that, even though the premise could have worked (I honestly do believe that), this is one of those shows that is probably better left forgotten.

But to steer away from the terribleness of it all, there is one interesting bit of trivia that goes along with this show - and you know you love some bits of trivia. Stand-up comic Stephanie Courtney had a small role on the show. Miss Courtney would become better known as Flo, the commercial spokesperson for Progressive Insurance, a competitor of the *Cavemen*'s own Geico. It's a small world, indeed...even if much of it is (rightfully) forgotten.

Pushing Daisies (2007-09)

Part Wes Anderson, part Tim Burton, with more than a touch of *Amélie*, this delightfully droll fantasy comedy-drama ran for two seasons on ABC from 2007 to 2009. The show was created by Bryan Fuller, the mad mind already behind such TV shows as *Dead Like Me* and *Wonderfalls*, and later on the man who brought both *Hannibal* and *American Gods* to television. Fuller was also the so-called deity behind the Fullerverse, the shared universe of all his shows, with characters from one show infiltrating another, creating a wider all-encompassing universe, much in the same manner of a Joss Whedon or a Quentin Tarantino.

The story of *Pushing Daisies* is simple. Ned is a pie maker who owns a shop called The Pie Hole. Great name. He has the ability to bring dead things back to life with but a touch. The catch being if they are back among the living for more than a minute, someone else in proximity will die in their place. This is what happened when childhood Ned brought back his mother after she dropped dead of an aneurysm. His neighbor's father dropped dead. Which was made doubly unfortunate as his now dead neighbor's daughter, Charlotte Charles, who he lovingly nicknamed Chuck, was the first and only girl poor hapless Ned ever loved. And then it was made triply unfortunate as his mother dropped dead again later that night when she kissed her son good night. This is when Ned found out a second touch kills the re-living again, and this time for reals.

Cut to many years later and we find Ned making pies in The Pie Hole (again, great name), and working with a private eye in solving crimes. Ned would bring the dead back for a minute and ask them who killed them before re-deading them, then collecting the reward money. The duo have a good gig going when a case comes in about a dead girl named Charlotte Charles. Ned hadn't seen his long lost love Chuck since the day of their parent's joint funeral. He brings her back to life, but can't send her back to the land of the dead, instead taking her home with him. The two fall in love, despite not being able to touch one another, and the duo of crime-solvers becomes a trio of crime-solvers, reluctantly so on the grumpy private eye's part. And this was all just in the first episode.

Lee Pace played the piemaker, a few years before he would become Ronan the Accuser in *Guardians of the Galaxy*. Anna Friel played Chuck and Chi McBride played private eye Emerson Cod. The show also featured Tony Award winner Kristen Chenoweth as Olive Snook, Ned's waitress at The Pie Hole (again, a great name), who also just so happened to be secretly in love with Ned. Chuck's agoraphobic aunts were played by Swoosie Kurtz and Ellen Greene. In keeping with the style of the show, each and every character was full of quirks. And speaking of the style of the show (and of the many quirks), *Pushing Daisies* was unlike pretty much anything on TV at the time.

As I said at the beginning, this show was designed to be part Tim Burton and part Wes Anderson, with more than a touch of the French comedy *Amélie*. The production design and cinematography of the show was quite kitschy and quite a lot of fun. By concentrating on contrasting colours and geometrical designs, production designer Michael Wylie told TV Guide that, "My goal was a storybook come to life. I wanted everything to look almost like an illustration." Cinematographer Michael Weaver told Variety that he and director Barry Sonnenfeld wanted the visuals to "feel somewhere between *Amélie* and a Tim Burton film – something big, bright and bigger than life." Symmetry was also a big aspect of the design of the show, both visually and in the writing. The palette full of reds and oranges, circles everywhere (representing possibly the circle of life, or perhaps just because circles look really cool), with criss cross patterns and stripes and checks and bright vivid colours abounding. Simply put, the show is gorgeous to look at. The show looked and felt like a fantasy, like a dream. With Sonnenfeld at the helm, his days of working with the Coen Brothers paid off.

And it wasn't just the look of the show. The fast paced dialogue, the use of an all-knowing narrator (voiced by the John Hurt sounding Jim Dale), the repetition of names (Charles Charles,

Boutique Travel Travel Boutique, The Darling Mermaid Darlings, and the town of Coeur d'Coeurs), the use of music (musical theater vets Chenowith and Greene both got to show off their song and dance chops on the show), and great performances all around made the show a critical hit. The show also was nominated for 17 Emmy Awards, winning seven of them. But alas, after a shortened nine episode first season (due to a writers strike) and just six episodes into an eventual thirteen episode second season, *Pushing Daisies* was cancelled. Although some things were wrapped up, the show never had a real conclusion. Fuller made attempts at continuing the series, his forensic fairy tale as it were, in the forms of comic books, a movie, and even a musical, but none of these ever came to fruition. Today, outside of the inevitable "shows gone too soon" articles, *Pushing Daisies* is but a faded memory of a short-lived but quite enjoyable television series.

Life on Mars (2008-09)

Life on Mars ran on ABC from October 9, 2008 to April 1, 2009, and was an American adaptation of the BAFTA winning UK series of the same name produced by the BBC. The premise was that of police detective Sam Tyler (played by Jason O'Mara, who was the voice of Batman in many an animated direct-to-video movie), who, after being struck by a car in 2008, wakes up in 1973, complete with all the proper period clothes and car and even a badge and I.D. that puts him in the same precinct as his 2008 counterpart had worked. Or is that, where his 2008 counterpart will work? Time travel is tricky ya know.

Anyway, the show had one of the more intriguing premises around. *Life on Mars,* deriving it's name from the David Bowie song which plays in both time periods in the series pilot, is a strange mélange indeed. Part *Law & Order*-esque police procedural, part *Mad Men* like nostalgia piece, part smoke and mirrors *Lost*-esque mystery. We watch as 2008 Sam Tyler traverses the landscape of his new 1973 world, trying to figure out how to get back to his own world. Along the way he comes face to face with his own mother and father, both currently around Sam's own age, as well as his own four year old self. There is also his hippie neighbour, who flits in and out of his daily life, and his new station mates at the old 125 precinct, which incidentally, in the most shocking shot of the entire show, rests in the shadow of the recently built and still standing tall World Trade Center.

These station mates include the gruff chief played by the venerable Harvey Keitel, a cocksure detective played by a brilliantly enjoyable, yet equally loathsome Michael Imperioli, his baby-faced partner played by Jonathan Murphy, and the put-upon police woman, played by Gretchen Mol, who dreams of becoming a detective and being taken seriously as a woman cop in the very sexist world of 1973. Sam struggles with this world that is so behind the more progressive world he was used too. But going along and fighting crime he does, never forgetting that he somehow needs to get home. All the while seeing glitches and flashes of his 2008 world. And then, seventeen episodes in, comes that ending. That twist ending.

So, since anyone could Google the ending of the UK series, which ended after two seasons just before it's American cousin took to the screen, the producers and writers wanted to do something different. And that they did. I don't want to spoil said ending for anyone here, because you need to see it to believe...and probably hate it too. There have been otherwise great shows ruined by a mediocre or rushed ending, both *Lost* and *Game of Thrones* come immediately to mind, but the finale of *Life on Mars* goes so far beyond those endings. So beyond. I realized that the ending needed to be rushed, due to getting cancelled with just one episode left to shove in everything they wanted to do, but the rush job on this finale was ridiculous. The show ran for seventeen episodes, which equaled about 734 minutes, and after 726 of those minutes, they decided to give us that aforementioned twist ending in the final 8 minutes of the season – which is like the show just gave everyone the finger.

The worst thing wasn't even the forced rush job. That was inevitable with the premature cancellation. The worst part was how much those last 8 minutes ruined the entirety of the show. The first sixteen episodes showed such great character development. Keitel took a seemingly stereotype and turned him into a multi-faceted character. Gretchen Mol took a scared little girl and developed her into a strong and successful detective. Imperioli, who's character never truly grows to be honest, is probably the deepest, truest character in the bunch. The way these actors and characters intertwined into each others lives, and the chemistry between them all was a wonder to watch with each and every episode. And then, in a mere eight minutes, that is all ruined. Everything leading up to this is made to not even matter, when we are given probably the worst ending in television history. It's as if that twist ending, and to be fair, I usually love twist endings, grabbed the rest of the series by the scruff of the neck (or maybe some other, more sensitive body part) and screamed, "Get lost punk! We don't need you anymore!" What a shame. What a real shame.

$#*! My Dad Says (2010-11)

There have been TV shows adapted from books and from plays, from movies and from magazine articles, from comics and from songs, from real life happenings or biographical subjects. Shows are sometimes even adapted from other shows, re the spinoff. Some shows just come out of thin air, essentially being adapted from nothing – just like *Seinfeld*, the show that was famously about nothing. There is even a show in this very book that was adapted from a TV commercial. But how many TV shows can you say were adapted from someone's Twitter feed? Well, here's one, but blink and you'll miss it – which most people did during its 18 episode run during the 2010-11 season.

Adapted from Justin Halpern's Twitter account called Shit My Dad Says, which is exactly what it sounds like, a Twitter feed of shit Justin Halpern's dad said. Anyhoo, David Kohan & Max Mutchnick, the creators of *Will & Grace*, took Halpern's Twitter feed and created a brand new sitcom for CBS. The producers hired the iconic William Shatner to play the shit talking dad, and away they went. Of course, a little manipulation of the name had to be done before cameras were allowed to roll, so *$#*! My Dad Says* (or *Bleep My Dad Says* in some circles) was born, and on September 23, 2010, it saw the so-called light of day. Eighteen weeks later it was sent to where the sun don't shine. To be honest, the show wasn't all that bad. It really wasn't all that good either, but it was far from the worst of television – or even the worst of this book.

The ratings were mediocre and the reviews were less than mediocre, and combine that with the difficulty of a simple little thing like talking about the show by name in commercials or print ads or on talk shows, and the show was never a hit like Halpern's trending Twitter feed had been. CBS had to quell every censor happy family group out there and reassure them that the V-Chip could block any hint of vulgarity their precious little cargo might hear. Shatner took a different approach, and just called people pussies for fearing the word shit. Of course, watching the show, you will see that all the vulgarity (or what certain people presume is vulgarity) inherent on Twitter, was edited out of the show's scripts, instead making Shatner's titular dad just another grumpy old man on a situation comedy. The show even won an award for Best New Comedy. Of course that was the People's Choice Awards, so it doesn't really count. Nonetheless, the prudish set persisted, and the show failed, and even though, as of the typing of these words, it hasn't even been a full decade since it left the air, all the $#*! Justin Halpern's Dad Said has been long forgotten.

Selfie (2014)

Debuting on ABC on September 30, 2014, *Selfie* was a modern day take on George Bernard Shaw's 1913 play, *Pygmalion*, which was later popularized by the 1956 stage musical and 1964 movie musical adaptation *My Fair Lady*, and had originally come from ancient Greek mythology. The story follows the daily life of Eliza Dooley, a junior executive at a big pharmaceutical company who is obsessed with social media and achieving her own sort of Kardashianesque fame via Instagram through her seemingly shallow (and quite constant) selfie awareness. Showing that she may not be quite as shallow as one would think, Eliza begins questioning her lifestyle, and seeks help from co-worker Henry Higgs, a marketing guru. Based, on Eliza Doolittle and Professor Henry Higgins from the aforementioned *My Fair Lady*, the show revolves around the Sam & Diane, will they or won't they relationship of these two characters, but in a modern self obsessed kinda way.

The show starred Karen Gillan as the intelligent yet rather flighty Eliza and John Cho as the sometimes too straight-laced Henry. Cho came into the show mainly known as one half of Harold & Kumar and as Lt. Sulu in JJ Abrams' new rebooted *Star Trek*. Gillan came aboard just after a three year run as Amy Pond, companion to the Eleventh Doctor on BBC's *Doctor Who*, and even more recently, balded and painted blue as Nebula in the first *Guardians of the Galaxy* film, released just a few months prior to *Selfie*'s debut. Gillan would go on to be in several of the Marvel Cinematic Universe movies, including *Avengers Endgame*, the top grossing film of all-time. But her future success on the big screen, nor her past success on the small screen (Amy Pond is one of *Doctor Who* fans' favourite characters), could not crossover into ratings for *Selfie*.

A dud from day one, at least ratings-wise, *Selfie* would be cancelled on November 7, 2014, after just six episodes. A week later, after the show's seventh episode aired, ABC announced the remaining six episodes would not appear on the network's fall schedule, but instead be released on Hulu and on other video on demand platforms. Personally, I found the show amusing. Perhaps not great, but still a fun show for what it was. Of course I would watch anything with Karen Gillan in it, even those awful *Jumanji* films she did. But alas, the show, predicated on an audience that needed to be of a younger mindset, the mindset that used Instagram and Snapchat and the like as their main source of social interaction, never caught on with the decidedly older crowd that actually still watched network programming in 2014. Maybe not the best, but not the worst show in this book either, but just like the one hundred mentioned before it, *Selfie* has surely been forgotten. Until now.

Conclusion

Well, that's it, but it's really not. There are so many other forgotten shows that could have been included here. Enough for two or three books. Even four or five. Too many to remember actually. See what I did there? Foreshadowed this book becoming a series. Yeah. Anyhoo, I digress. As I was concluding, there are so many other shows that could have been included in this book. It was actually quite difficult to narrow it down. I ended up leaving out shows such as the godawful *Delta House*, a short lived attempt at recreating the energy of *Animal House* on the smaller screen. I left out *Poochinski*, a failed pilot for a cop show where gruff cop Peter Boyle is killed and reincarnated as a flatulent bull dog. I left out *Big Bad Beetleborgs*, a blatant rip-off of the *Mighty Morphin Power* Rangers. I left out *The Greatest American Hero*, a show whose theme song can be sung in full by pretty much anyone of Generation X, but is pretty much forgotten in every other aspect. Yeah, I left out a lot, but that only gives me more fodder for future volumes of Forgotten TV.

My advice to all those faithful readers who got this far in the book (even those who skipped ahead) is to get out there and check out some of these shows. From the good shows (*Voyage to the Bottom of the Sea, The Goldbergs, Fridays, Sports Night*) to the godawful shows (*Manimal, Woops!*, that hideous Hitler sitcom), most can be found in some form or another either online or on DVD. Even the godawful ones are worth a watch – even if it is just for an unsolicited laugh. See for yourself and make your own judgments. Maybe then, these shows will be a little less forgotten. Goodbye for now. See y'all in my next book.

Fin.

www.ingramcontent.com/pod-product-compliance
Lightning Source LLC
Chambersburg PA
CBHW051048160426
43193CB00010B/1105